@Copyright 2020by Wallace Buendia - **All rights reserved.**

This document is geared towards providing exact and reliable information in regards to the topic and issue covered. The publication is sold with the idea that the publisher is not required to render accounting, officially permitted, or otherwise, qualified services. If advice is necessary, legal or professional, a practiced individual in the profession should be ordered.

Under no circumstance will any legal responsibility or blame be held against the publisher for any reparation, damages, or monetary loss due to the information herein, either directly or indirectly.

Legal Notice:

The book is copyright protected. This is only for personal use. You cannot amend, distribute, sell, use, quote or paraphrase any part or the content within this book without the consent of the author.

Disclaimer Notice:

Please note the information contained within this document is for educational and entertainment purposes only. Every attempt has been made to provide accurate, up to date and reliable complete information. No warranties of any kind are expressed or implied. Readers acknowledge that the author is not engaging in the rendering of legal, financial, medical or professional advice. The content of this book has been derived from various sources. Please consult a licensed professional before attempting any techniques outlined in this book.

CONTENTS

INTRODUCTION 6
    What makes the Ninjaz Foody incredible? 8

CHAPTER ONE WHAT IS THE NINJAZ FOODY GRILL AND HOW IT WORKS 9
    How does the Ninjaz Foody Grill look and feel? 9
    What can the Ninjaz Foody Grill do? 10
    What we like 10
    How can it perform? 10
    Air Frying 11
    Roasting 11
    Baking 11
    Getting dried out 11
    Is the Ninjaz Foody Grill simple to utilize and clean? 12
    Guarantee 12
    Is the Ninjaz Foody Grill justified? 12
    What the Ninjaz Foody Does 12
    The following highlights are used with the pressure cooking cover on. 13
    The following component is utilized without a top on the Ninjaz Foody 13
    The following highlights are utilized with the crisping cover on. 13
    The following component is just on specific models and is utilized with the crisping top on. 13
    Where the Ninjaz Foody can improve 14
    How it compares to competitor 14
    Is the Ninjaz Foody worth the cost? 15
    What cooking presets are accessible on the Ninjaz Foody? 15
    Time and temp settings 16
    What does the guarantee on the Ninjaz Foody cover? 16
    What Comes With The Ninjaz Foody? 18
    Beginning With the Ninjaz Foody 20
    The most effective method to Use the Ninjaz Foody And Its Various Functions 21
    Choosing the Right Time for Pressure Cooking? 22
    How much Liquid Can We Use When Pressure Cooking? 22
    Would it be a good idea for me to Use the Basket or Rack When Air Frying? 25
    How can I Convert Instant Pot Recipes for The Ninjaz Foody? 27

CHAPTER TWO SCRUMPTIOUS BREAKFAST DISHES FOR YOUR GRILL 28

- Grilled Bacon-and-Herb Grit Cakes 28
- Open-air fire Fried Eggs with Potato-and-Bacon Hash 28
- Grilled Apricots with Brie, Prosciutto, and Honey 29
- Grilled French toast with Strawberries and Rosemary 30
- Grilled Breakfast Pizza 30
- Grilled bruschetta portobello mushrooms 31
- Avocado Eggs on the Grill 33
- Eggs Benedict Burger 33
- Shakshuka 34
- Grilled Fried Eggs 35
- Omelet on the Grill 36
- Grilled Breakfast Casserole 37
- Grilled Hash Browns 38
- Campfire French Toast 38
- Coconut French Toast with Grilled Pineapple 39
- Grilled Sausages 39
- Grilled Fruit Packets 40
- Grilled French toast Kebabs 40
- Farmhouse Breakfast 41
- Plum-Glazed Sausage 42
- Grilled Peaches with Honey 42
- Grilled Breakfast Burrito 43

CHAPTER THREE GRILLED RECIPES FOR DINNER 44

- Steak Fajitas 44
- Grilled Shrimp and Tomatoes with Linguine 45
- Chili Rubbed Ribs 46
- Grilled Garden Veggie Pizza 47
- Firecracker Grilled Salmon 47
- Steak and New Potato Toss 48
- Grilled Pork Noodle Salad 49
- Chicken with Peach-Cucumber Salsa 50
- Meat and Potato Kabobs 50
- Garden Fish Tacos 51
- Steak with Chipotle-Lime Chimichurri 51
- Rosemary-Lemon Grilled Chicken 52
- Beef and Blue Cheese Penne with Pesto 53
- Chicken Alfredo with Grilled Apples 53
- Quick Cajun Chicken Penne 54
- Creamy Herb-Grilled Herb - Grilled Salmon 54
- Zesty Grilled Chops 55
- Chicken and Vegetable Kabobs 55
- Saucy Grilled Baby Back Ribs 56
- Grilled Steak Bruschetta Salad 56
- Maple-Thyme Chicken Thighs 57
- Grilled Steak Salad with Tomatoes and Avocado 57

Delicate Pork Chops with Mango Salsa 58
Grilled Shrimp and Peach Kabobs 58
Southwest Steak and Potatoes 59
Salmon Salad with Glazed Walnuts 59
Portobello Fajitas 60
Ginger Halibut with Brussels Sprouts 60
Grilled Huli Huli Chicken 61
Honey Glazed Chicken Kabobs 61
Grilled Tilapia Piccata 62
Honey-Chipotle Ribs 62
Grilled Veggie Pizza 63
Brown Sugar Salmon with Strawberries 63
Lemon Chicken Skewers 64
Maple and Blue Cheese Steak 64
Lime-Glazed Pork Chops 65
Steak Kabobs 66
Blackened Chicken 66
Barbeque Alaskan Salmon 67
Butterly Grilled Shrimp 67
Blue Cheese Flat Iron Steak 68
Ricotta-Stuffed Portobello Mushrooms 69
Grilled Greek Pita Pizzas 69
Grilled Tilapia with Pineapple Salsa 70
Spicy Barbecued Chicken 70
CHAPTER FOUR GRILLED APPETIZER RECIPES 71
Grilled Appetizer Party Pointers 71
Grilled Tequila-Lime Shrimp 71
Thai Chicken Satay 72
Pesto-Stuffed Grilled Portobellos 72
Grilled Eggplant Rollups 73
Grilled Prosciutto and Peach Flatbread Pizza 74
Grilled Tofu Skewers with Sriracha Sauce 74
Grill Master Chicken Wings 75
Marinated Chicken Kabobs 75
Steak on a Stick 76
Strawberry Goat Cheese Bruschetta 77
Shrimp and Scallops with Lemony Soy 77
Grilled-Vegetable Gazpacho 78
Sausage Lovers' Grilled Pizza 79
Smoking' Sweet Chicken Wings with Cherry Barbecue Glaze 80
Grilled Beef Rolls 81
Grilled Tomato Crostini 82
Spiced Shrimp and Tomato Kebabs 82
Grilled Apricot, Arugula, and Goat Cheese Salad 83
Pork Satay 84
Grilled Oysters with Chorizo Butter 85
CHAPTER FIVE GRILLED RECIPES FOR VEGETARIAN, FISH, AND SEAFOODS 86

Grilled Eggplant, Roasted Red Pepper Sandwich, and Halloumi 86
Grilled Tofu Tacos with Avocado Cashew Cream 86
Grilled Eggplant with Herbed Quinoa 88
Grilled Tofu and Soba Noodles Recipe 89
Fish and Seafood Grilled Onion-Butter Cod 90
Moroccan Grilled Fish Kebabs 91
Grilled Bacon-Wrapped Scallops with Lemon Aioli 92
Tuna Chops with Lemon Cream Sauce 93
Grilled Dungeness Crab 94
Grilled Sea Bass Marinated 95
Lime and Basil Tilapia Recipe 95
Grilled Scallops with Mango/Peaches and Red Bell Pepper 96
Cilantro Lime Fish Halibut 97

CHAPTER SIX ONE WEEK OF GRILLED MEAL PLAN 98
What's Included 98
No Breakfasts or Lunches? 99
Uncommon Notes Regarding This Grilling Meal Plan: 99
What to Buy 100
Produce 100
Pantry 102
Meat 103
One Week Grilling Meal Plan: Dinners 103

INTRODUCTION

The Ninjaz Foody grill guarantees that children can get their grilled foods regardless of whether it's 32 degrees with freezing precipitation outside. In any case, in particular, its flexibility past grilling makes it a family cooking machine practically perfect for families with kids — regardless of whether they like grilled foods or not. A foot and half long and 14 inches wide, the Foody grill is entirely minimal for squeezed kitchen spaces. What's more, to be completely forthright, when I initially set it on my counter, I was somewhat questionable that the ten by 10-inch high-thickness grill mesh would be large enough for my family's grilled meat needs. In any case, I found that it could cook four pork cleaves at once without swarming. Considering there are four individuals at the table each night, that was genuinely great.The Ninjaz Foody grill works by warming up the grill addition to a rankling 500 degrees. That hot grill plate joined with a convection framework that courses the air implies food prepares rapidly and falls off the grill pleasantly seared and fresh, complete with the restaurant denote that demonstrate your work. This arrangement of air and warmth, alongside the capacity to control cooking temperature, additionally implies that you can grill regardless of whether your food is solidified. That sort of accommodation is incredible for occupied families. Having the option to plunge into the cooler and grill without defrosting is a major in addition to it.One thing we may stress over before utilizing the Foody grill was that it would clear my family out of the house. Be that as it may, smoke is moderated by circling the air, and oil watch, and a "cool air zone." I don't know how everything attempts to prevent the thing from spilling

out smoke, yet I cooked an inexorably oily choice of meats, generally without inconvenience. The one time I got cleared out was the point at which I fail to clean the 6-quart inset before grilling the second cluster of frankfurters. The smoke was overpowering. However, it was additionally because of the client's mistake. Each time I've utilized the prescribed oil and began with a perfect machine, the smoke has never been an issue.

If the Foody was only a grill, It is considered as a "decent to have" kitchen embellishment for families. Also, the Foody can likewise go about as an air fryer, a dehydrator, an iron, and a roaster. You can likewise utilize it to prepare. However, that assignment is by all accounts for increasingly master clients. That flexibility drives the device over the line into "must-have" an area. After cooking on the Ninjaz Foody grill, what thrills me is that it is so cordial to kiddie foods. It wrenches out immaculate grilled sausages, and the iron frill can take out sure pancakes. Fly in the discretionary lack of hydration rack for some dried natural product snacks, and you have a damn child-driven kitchen cooker.Likewise, similar to the Instant Pot, the Ninjaz Foody Grill requires some an opportunity to preheat before you can begin cooking. That preheat time doesn't generally protract supper prep to an extreme, taking into account how rapidly it grills. In any case, no one jumps at the chance to pause. Figure out how to prepare the ingredients during preheat time. If you happen to have an Instant Pot in your home, at that point, the Ninjaz Foody Grill will be an invite expansion to your multicooker weapons store. Also, honestly, between the two, you may go a long time between turning on your stovetop or oven. What's more, perhaps that interests you. I realize what requests to me: The Ninjaz

Foody Grill is a child's food preparing machine — something I never realized I required and now something I can't survive without. It's the kitchen MVP.The Ninjaz Foody Grill. The grill that burns, sizzles, and air fry crisps. Indoor grill and air fryer500F air circles around food for stunning Surround Searing while the 500F high-thickness grill grind makes burn grilled stamps and flavors, for food that is splendidly cooked within and singe grilled on each side with Cyclonic Grilling TechnologyWith the BTU cooking intensity of an outside grill, it brings open-air grill enhances helpfully to your ledge any day of the yearForgot to defrost supper? Change foods from solidified to scorch grilled in a short time splendidlyAir cook fresh with to 75% less fat than profound searing (tried against hand-cut, pan-fried French fries), utilizing the included 4-qt crisper bin1760-watt unit; 10" x 10" PTFE/PFOA free, nonstick, fired covered grill grind; 4-qt PTFE/ PFOA open, nonstick, clay-covered crisper container; 6-qt PTFE/ PFOA free, nonstick, earthenware included cooking pot; Chef-made 15-recipe book; Cleaning brushWe've heard a lot of promotion about the Ninjaz Foody in the quest for an air fryer and additionally pressure cooker, however now you're thinking about whether it satisfies it.

You could pore over endless audits on the web. However, that gets overpowering genuine fast. Along these lines, we did it for you. Do you know how the Instant Pot professes to be a one-stop search for the entirety of your cooking machine needs? The Ninjaz Foody makes that a stride further by joining the intensity of a multi cooker with an air fryer. The Foody can pressure cook, slow cook, sauté, steam, and air fry. It additionally includes Tender Crisp innovation, which is a mix of weight cooking and air singing that enables you to cook ingredients and polish off with a firm surface quickly. An Instant Pot can't do that. Note that this component makes the Ninjaz Foody stand apart from the group. Owning a Foody should untether you from having three separate appliances (a pressure cooker, a moderate cooker, and an air fryer.) It takes up more space than an Instant Pot or an air fryer all alone, yet in general, it diminishes mess.

What makes the Ninjaz Foody incredible?

Most importantly, the way that it replaces more than one machine is gigantic in addition to — that is the reason we cherished the Instant Pot, so a lot of when it turned out. What's more, even though it has a tremendous amount of employment, it doesn't compromise on any of them. "The Foody is shockingly simple to utilize and doesn't hold back on viability in pressing in its extensive rundown of capacities."Cooking with the Foody is idiot-proof, regardless of whether you need to make a flavorful pork tenderloin that self-destructs with a jab of your fork, or sweet potato fries that are crunchy outwardly and fleecy on the inside. It's straightforward for dishes, sides, treats, or whatever else you can think to cook with it. Regardless of whether you're not an expert or following the included recipe manage, Good Housekeeping says the controls are clear and intuitive to utilize. The situation of the Foody's weight discharge valves is marked, and the control board includes simple to-utilize catches with presets and custom settings.

CHAPTER ONE WHAT IS THE NINJAZ FOODY GRILL AND HOW IT WORKS

Indeed, even in the most sorted out and exclusive kitchens, it's challenging to prepare for single-reason ledge appliances. So frequently, you'll utilize an item a bunch of times, just to consign the massive one-stunt horse to the storage room, the upper room, or even the yard sale. However, items that can accomplish more than a single thing, and do them well, might merit giving a changeless home on your ledge.The most up to date gadget clamoring for space? The Ninjaz Foody Grill, one of the most up to date augmentations to a developing biological system of Foody items. Notwithstanding grilling, it can likewise air fry, heat, cook, and get dried out. Here's the lowdown on whether it merits heaps of cash it's presently selling for—or whether you'd be in an ideal situation with another of our preferred indoor grills.

How does the Ninjaz Foody Grill look and feel?

The Ninjaz Foody Grill is vast, and it's square-shaped—7 inches in length by 14 inches wide by 11 inches tall. Giving you an idea of exactly how huge that is, envision an across the board printer, or an enormous bread box. The grill is built of brushed tempered steel and has a dark plastic domed top.While this Ninjaz won't win any magnificence challenges, despite everything, it has a pleasant completion and top-notch feel. It's additionally very overwhelming, so you won't have any desire to lift it all through a bureau all the time.With the grill, you get a robust grill grind, a crisper bushel, and a cooking pot that are altogether covered with a clay nonstick completion. A cleaning brush and kebab sticks are additionally included.

What can the Ninjaz Foody Grill do?

It can grill, air fry, broil, heat, and dry out.As you would envision, this Foody can grill. Even though it cooks with the top shut, the cover doesn't push down on food, so it just brands grill blemishes on each side in turn—if you need a panini, you'll need to turn it over partially through cooking. The mesh leaves bent grill stamps as opposed to straight lines on food.Notwithstanding grilling, the Ninjaz Food Grill can air fry, broil, prepare, and get dried out, which covers a significant number of the elements of the Ninjaz Foody Pressure Cooker and Ninjaz Foody Oven.

What we like

- It's all around developed.The digital controls are anything but difficult to peruse and intuitive to explore.It's fantastic at grilling—and it doesn't deliver smoke.It additionally utilized for air browning, roasting, baking, and getting dried out.

What we don't care for

- It's costly.It's enormous.The preheat times for grilling are long.The grill marks are blended.There could be all the more cooking rules for specific capacities in the cookbook.

How can it perform?

GrillingTo test the grilling capacity, we cooked both new and solidified burgers, chicken bosoms, salmon, and New York strip steaks—and we were exceptionally dazzled. The chicken and burgers appeared as though they could have been done on an open-air grill. The skin on the salmon was magnificently fresh and the top very much seared, even without flipping.While the strip steaks didn't equal those grilled outside, they turned out superior to anything numerous steaks cooked in an oven. Even though the preheat time for grilling was around eight minutes, the food prepared rapidly once on.Our preferred piece of the grilling experience? The Ninjaz was completely smokeless all through.

Air Frying

The Foody Grill equals the best air fryers we've tried. Both new and solidified fries turned out near those cheap food ones that we as a whole find so overwhelming. On most air fryers, you pull out a container to thrash around foods during searing, and it very well may be clumsy to hold the bin as you work. In any case, as the Ninjaz's cover opens upwards, we thought that it was' straightforward to get to things that should be flipped in the crisper bushel.

Roasting

If you don't care for turning on your oven, you can cook a little cut of meat on the Ninjaz Grill. A pork flank broil turned out delicate and delicious with a snapping outside layer.

Baking

You can even heat a cake in the Foody Grill, as the cooking pot is sufficiently huge to hold an 8-inch container. In any case, don't expect completely flawless outcomes. A yellow cake turned out equally seared with a clammy delicate morsel. However, it was genuinely domed and split on top.If you don't have a full-size oven at your administration and aren't excessively particular about how your prepared merchandise looks, this grill could be a fast method to get a handcrafted dessert on the table.

Getting dried out

I was intrigued with how well the Foody Grill got dried out, turning out apple rings that were the ideal level of chewiness in seven hours. Nonetheless, you can just fit around 18 cuts onto the Foody at once, which yields about a cup and a portion of dried apple rings.If you love making your own dried organic products, even in little bits, and are eager to leave an apparatus working throughout the day or medium-term, you'll be content with the outcomes.

Is the Ninjaz Foody Grill simple to utilize and clean?

The Foody is well-structured, and every single removable part is dishwasher safe. The digital control board on the grill is very much structured and simple to peruse. We love the way that the grill preheats; consequently, however relying upon the setting, the preheat time can be more than eight minutes.In the highest point of the top, there's a splatter shield that should be jumped out after each utilization and cleaned. Fortunately, the entirety of the removable parts (counting the guard) can go in the dishwasher. The inside and outside of the machine don't get especially grimy and are anything but difficult to clean off.The Ninjaz Foody grill accompanies an intensive and straightforward proprietor's guide, just as a booklet that contains recipes and cooking graphs for grilling, air singing, and getting dried out. The main things it's missing are rules for baking and roasting.

Guarantee

Ninjaz offers a one-year restricted warranty on the Foody Grill and a 60-day cash back guarantee. People rave about its grilling and air searing execution and love the way that it's smokeless. However, they do say that it's a "monster kitchen thing" and that it's substantial, so they expected to locate a committed spot for it.

Is the Ninjaz Foody Grill justified?

Any individual who adores grilled foods yet doesn't have simple access to an open-air grill will cherish this Ninjaz. It tans food much superior to an oven, and not at all like skillet grilling won't top off your home with smoke. The way that it can likewise air fry is a major in addition to. While it similarly cooks, heats, and gets dried out, we wouldn't run out and get it for those abilities.You need to remember that you'll require an enormous space in your kitchen or a close-by storeroom to oblige this Foody—yet for good grilling, it merits the capacity.

What the Ninjaz Foody Does

If you aren't sure precisely what a Ninjaz Foody is or are uncertain pretty much the entirety of its highlights, here is a short depiction of what it does. A Ninjaz Foody with Tender Crisp innovation is an electric kitchen apparatus that capacities as a multi-use cooker. Its two major highlights are pressure cooker and air fryer. However, it additionally accomplishes such a great deal more. Here are the highlights:

The following highlights are used with the pressure cooking cover on.

Pressure Cooker: The Pressure cooking capacity can be set to High or Low, and you can redo the time that you need the food to prepare as long as 4 hours. When utilizing the weight cooking capacity, you will turn the dark valve on the highest point of the Foody to seal.**Steam:** There is no temperature modification when utilizing the steam setting. You can alter the time for as long as 30 minutes. When using this component, it is critical to ensure the dark valve on the top is set to vent and not to seal.**Slow Cook:** This capacity works as a moderate cooker would and can be set to High or Low. You can modify the time as long as 12 hours. When utilizing this component, you will need the dark valve on the top set to vent and not to seal.

The following component is utilized without a top on the Ninjaz Foody

Burn/Sauté: This component has different temperature settings; High, Med-Hi, Med, Med-Low, and low. You don't be able to set the ideal opportunity for this element. It will remain on until you turn it off. You can utilize the weight top with the sauté capacity even though I prescribe utilizing the singe/sauté without a cover so you can watch out for your food effectively.

The following highlights are utilized with the crisping cover on.

The Tender Crisp Technology: The Air Crisp capacity has temperature settings from 300º F to 400° F, and you can tweak the time as long as 60 minutes.**Bake Roast:** The bake feature has temperature settings from 250° F up to 400º F, and you can tweak the time as long as 4 hours.**Broil:** The Broil Function doesn't have a temperature modification; it is either on or off. You can alter the time for as long as 30 minutes.

The following component is just on specific models and is utilized with the crisping top on.

Lack of hydration: The parchedness work enables you to change the temperature from 105° F to 195º F. You can modify the time from 15 minutes as long as 12 hours.

Where the Ninjaz Foody can improve

While the Ninjaz Foody is exceptional in vast amounts of classes, there are two or three territories where it could be better. The greatest grievance across surveys is the cover circumstance. Since the Foody is two distinct appliances, it needs two unique covers to complete the capacities. The searing air top is connected through a pivot, and the weight cooking cover is removable, becoming an integral factor just when you need it. While the considerable air searing top swings open to be to some degree off the beaten path while pressure cooking, it's not the best structure."When utilizing the weight cooker, we ended up wishing we could expel the air fricasseeing top. It only sort of stays there, and it's overwhelming and unbalanced while you pressure cook."Numerous individuals additionally call attention to that the Ninjaz Foody is unimaginably cumbersome, and keeping in mind that it takes the spot of different appliances, it's as yet not an excessively advantageous machine to store.

How it compares to competitor

The Ninjaz Foody is bulkier and more substantial than other multicookers and air fryers, however on the off chance that you can look past that, it beats its rivals.Analysts rave about the delicacy of dishes they cooked under tension, and the firmness of their air seared food or those polished off with the Tender Crisp setting. As far as food quality, the Foody positions up as well as anyone.This machine is more straightforward to clean than an Instant Pot as a result of the covering on the inner pot and the Foody's plastic outside. The simplicity of cleaning, except with regards to the air singing cover: Since it's associated with the machine and has a mesh that is difficult to get into, it's a huge problem to clean.Concerning highlights, the Foody honestly can do everything a standard Instant Pot can do. The additional air singing usefulness makes the Ninjaz Foody a champion machine that doesn't generally have many direct examination competitors right now.

Is the Ninjaz Foody worth the cost?

The Foody's capacities don't come modest — the apparatus retails for $249.99. Is it justified, however? In case you're going to utilize it. Usually, the agreement is by all accounts, yes. If you are huge into multi cooking and air singing, it's certainly valuable to have quite recently the one apparatus that does all that you need.

What cooking presets are accessible on the Ninjaz Foody?

While some home cooks may joyfully depend on presets on their pressure cookers, the adaptable open alternatives on the Ninjaz Foody make it entirely incredible. You essentially need to cause notes as you go on to what extent various foodstuffs take to cook, and you'll be pressure concocting a storm in a matter of seconds by any means. While the Ninjaz Foody doesn't have any pre-customized presets, yet it has up to eight diverse cooking modes. For the ideal outcomes, it's essential to comprehend what everyone does and how to utilize them appropriately. The cooking choices on a Ninjaz Foody are as per the following:

- **Pressure:** Use to prepare food rapidly while looking after delicacy.**Steam:** Use to tenderly cook raw foods, for example, fish or vegetables at high temperatures.**Slow cook:** Cooks food like soup or stews at a lower temperature for longer periods.**Sear/sauté:** This lets you utilize your Foody as a stovetop for searing meats, sautéing vegetables, or stewing sauces.**Air fresh:** This is the Ninjaz Foody as an air fryer, meaning you can cook things like fries utilizing just a modest quantity of oil.**Bake/cook:** This is the setting to use to broil meat or make bread, cakes, and other heated things.**Broil:** Use this choice to caramelize and darker your food.
- **Dehydrate (just on explicit models):** Dehydrate meats, organic produce, and vegetables.

It might take some altering. However, you'll get extraordinary outcomes once you've aced your Ninjaz Foody. With experimentation, you may even discover you want to utilize elective settings. For instance, you may pick to pressure certain cook vegetables, as opposed to using the steam cooking mode.

Time and temp settings

When you select the cooking mode you need, you essentially need to set up the planning and temperature choices. You can utilize the here and their TEMP bolts to set the temperature, at that point, utilize the all over TIME bolts to choose to what extent you'd like your food to prepare for.Specific Ninjaz Foody cooking modes, for example, the weight cooking alternative, will actuate the cooker's helpful "Keep Warm" mode. When your recipe's cook time is done, the unit will blare and naturally change to its "Keep Warm" setting. It starts another clock, so you realize to what extent your food has been resting.If the idea of utilizing weight and slow cooker without worked in presets fills you with culinary worry, there is a lot of counsel online to assist you with acing the uncertain time'n'temp balance. Start little with essential recipes, however consistently watch that any food, particularly meat, is cooked through. Nobody likes chicken on the pink side.If you are as yet sold on presets, the Ninjaz Foody may not be the best fit for you. Even though it is conceivable to show signs of improvement quality outcomes with a little experimentation, the Foody simply doesn't have those presets. On the off chance that you aren't feeling the motivation and you need those preset choices, the Instant Pot may be a superior choice for your kitchen. In any case, these stunning kitchen devices make cooking way easier...and scrumptious.

What does the guarantee on the Ninjaz Foody cover?

Ninjaz Foody isn't modest, so you have to realize you're secured in case you're sufficiently unfortunate to have yours separate. At the point when you buy a Foody, you have a composed assurance, or guarantee, from the producer that vows to repair or supplant the item inside a particular period. On account of the Ninjaz Foody, that period is one year. This guarantee covers the genuine Ninjaz Foody, not the removable parts.This works when you keep the receipt. Continuously keep the receipt or some evidence of procurement for your Ninjaz Foody. This will be significant should you have to guarantee on the guarantee. Your guarantee isn't substantial if you can't give verification of procurement. You can make a beeline for the Ninjaz Kitchen bolster site or call to address a client assistance body and start a guarantee. There are approaches to void the warranty, so here are things to maintain a strategic distance from.Out karmaThe Ninjaz Foody guarantee just covers multicookers that have been utilized in what the organization calls "typical family unit conditions."

Your warranty doesn't include any sort of expert or business utilization of your cooker. Additionally, keep it clean. You can nullify your warranty on the off chance that you don't shield the engine base from fluids, food spills, and different trash.If your Foody goes wonky, don't, under any conditions, endeavor to repair it yourself or get another person to investigate it. Your guarantee isn't legitimate if the unit has been messed with. The maker expresses that "modifying, or repairing the Shark Ninjaz item (or any of its parts) when the repair is performed by a repair individual not

approved by Shark Ninjaz" voids your assurance.Pot karmaSadly, however, the guarantee covers any item breakdowns, it doesn't cover everything. The warranty doesn't cover typical mileage of wearable parts, for example, removable pots, racks, and skillet. If you wear those out, your lone choice is to purchase new pieces from the Ninjaz Accessories store.**Ninjaz Foody model number OP300–**This is a 6.5 quart model WITHOUT the parchedness work.

- 1400-watt unitPressure topCrisping top6.5-quart clay covered potStainless steel reversible rack4-quart clay included Cook and Crisp Basket

Ninjaz Foody model number OP301–This is a 6.5 quart model WITHOUT the lack of hydration work.

- 1400-watt unitPressure coverCrisping cover6.5-quart earthenware covered potStainless steel reversible rack4-quart earthenware referred Cook and Crisp Basket

Ninjaz Foody model number OP301C-This is a 6.5 quart model WITH the drying out capacity.

- 1400-watt unitPressure coverCrisping cover6.5-quart earthenware covered potStainless steel reversible steam/sear rack4-quart earthenware referred Cook and Crisp BasketCook and Crisp Layered Insert

Ninjaz Foody model number OP302–This is the 6.5 quart model WITH the drying out capacity.

- 1400-watt unitPressure coverCrisping cover6.5-quart earthenware covered potStainless steel reversible steam/sear rack4-quart earthenware referred Cook and Crisp Basket

Ninjaz Foody model number OP305–This is the 6.5 quart model WITH the drying out capacity.

- 1400-watt unitPressure coverCrisping cover6.5-quart earthenware covered potStainless steel reversible steam/sear rack4-quart earthenware referred Cook and Crisp BasketCook and Crisp Layered Insert

Ninjaz Foody model number OP401–This is the 8 quart model WITH the drying out capacity. The main distinction between model 302 and 401 is quart size and a higher wattage.

- 1700-watt unitPressure coverCrisping coverXL 8-quart earthenware covered potStainless steel reversible rackXL 5-quart earthenware referred Cook and Crisp BasketCook and Crisp Layered Insert

Ninjaz Foody model number FD402–This is the most current 8 quart model WITH the lack of hydration work and a yogurt work. It has a sleeker structure and a handle that chooses different capacities rather than catches.

- 1760-watt unitPressure coverCrisping coverXL 8-quart fired covered potThe stainless steel deluxe reversible rack with two layersXL 5-quart fired covered Cook and Crisp Basket

What Comes With The Ninjaz Foody?

Your Ninjaz Foody will land in a huge box, which is relatively overwhelming, so be cautious lifting it. There is a subsequent box, and inside that container is the real Ninjaz Foody. Everything is bundled very well for transportation.

A Ninjaz Foody Cookbook: There is a cookbook with more than 45 recipes to get you started. Additionally remembered for the back are outlines that give you rules for cooking with various settings and timing for different foods. I have gotten notification from various individuals that the recipes in the book will, in general, be salty, so utilize your judgment with the flavoring suggestions. I have just attempted the Macaroni and Cheese recipe, and I need to state it was loathsome. I even cut a path back on the salt despite everything it was unappetizing. If you make it, forget about the baking soft drink as I imagine that was the guilty party. They added the baking soft drinks to protect the surface of the noodles. However, it truly gave the entire dish a peculiar taste. If you have attempted any of them if it's not too much trouble, leave us to remark with your musings on the recipe in the remark segment at the base of this post. That way, everybody can share and gain from one another. **Know your Foody guide:** This is a speedy beginning aide that quickly clarifies what's in the case and why there are two covers, diagrams the weight test and works, and incorporates a cooking cheat sheet. There is additionally a recipe for an entire simmered chicken that looks fabulous. **Owners Guide:** This is an exhaustive manual for utilizing your Foody and incorporates an outline of the different elements of the Ninjaz Foody, goes over consideration and support of the Foody, and includes an investigating guide. I do suggest perusing the proprietor's control when

you initially begin with the Ninjaz Foody. **Pressure Cooker Lid:** This is a different cover that you will put on when utilizing various capacities on the Ninjaz Foody. On the underside of this cover is a valve top, this top can and ought to be expelled for cleaning after each utilization. The dark valve over the Ninjaz Foody can be evacuated by the proprietors' control for cleaning and reviewing for obstructs. At the point when my Foody was conveyed, the dark valve top was off. I had the option to pop it back on effectively and have not had any issues. The valve should be free and buoy when on the seal. This is wellbeing insurance, so overabundance steam/weight can be discharged during pressure cooking. At the point when you turn the valve to vent, it rises a piece and sits on a little edge.

You will feel it fit properly. If your dark top falls off, simply pop it back on. There is likewise a red catch on the highest point of the weight top. This catch remains discouraged until the Ninjaz Foody comes up to weight, and afterward, it springs up. You can't open the cover when the red trick is up. This is a wellbeing highlight to forestall cracking the pot while it is feeling the squeeze that could bring about consumes.**Air Crisp Lid:** The air fresh cover remains connected to the Ninjaz Foody, and you put it down over the pot during specific cooking capacities. It has a fan and a warming component. The fan circles the sight-seeing like a convection oven. You can open the cover whenever during the cooking procedure to mind your food.

Beginning With the Ninjaz Foody

Before First Use:

After you have unloaded the Ninjaz Foody, you will need to wash the launderable parts thoroughly. I prescribe utilizing the dishwasher to remove the silicone ring (on the top rack), the container, stand, and the inward pot. Never put the weight cooker top or the Ninjaz Foody base in the dishwasher. I have perused where many individuals will wash their weight cooker top in the dishwasher. However, I don't suggest it. There is additionally a silver enemy of stop up top within the weight cooker cover that can (and should) be evacuated and cleaned before the primary use and after each utilization. I prescribe washing this by hand, and a toothbrush works extraordinary. The counter obstructs the top shields the internal pressure valve from getting stopped up. If the inward valve is stopped up, you may see food splashing out of the discharge valve when you discharge the weight. I have never seen any food or debris and jetsam on my enemy to stop up top, yet it is as yet a smart thought to clean it. There is additionally a buildup plate that should be set up before first use. This doesn't influence the way the Ninjaz Foody works. However, gather any buildup that may create during weight or steam cooking. Make sure to expel it and clean it after each utilization. However, I have heard a few anecdotes about form developing when the water isn't exhausted out. You possibly need to stress over this when cooking with the weight cover on. Buildup won't shape when the delicate fresh coat is being used.

Pressure Test:

At the point when you initially get your Ninjaz Foody, you will need to acclimate yourself with it and ensure it is filling in as expected. The non-demanding approach to do this is by directing a Pressure Test. The pressure test is straightforward. You will add three cups of water to the inward pot, secure the weight cover, turn the dark valve to seal. Press the Pressure Button, select high with the bolts to one side, and choose 3 minutes with the bolts to one side — hit start. You will see a pivoting square of lights telling you that the Ninjaz Foody is warming up. This can take 8-10 minutes. The Ninjaz Foody needs to warm the water to make the steam expected to go under pressure. During this time, you may see steam getting away from the dark valve as well as the red catch on the highest point of the cover. This is typical. On the off chance that you see steam turning out around the entire lid, this isn't typical. Stop the Ninjaz Foody. Turn the dark valve to vent and enable the steam to get away. Evacuate the cover and will allow it to cool. The most widely recognized explanation this happens is the seal isn't accurately put. Ensure the silicone seal is situated in the furrows of the pressure cooker top.

The most effective method to Use the Ninjaz Foody And Its Various Functions

Pressure Cooker Function:

The weight cooker is a pot with a fixing cover that has a valve (the dark valve that abandons seal to vent) to discharge pressure and a vent/button (the red button) to control pressure. With the end goal, we will allude an electric weight cooker like the Ninjaz Foody. The weight cooking highlight is an extraordinary method to accelerate the cooking procedure. Instant Pot entire Chicken Foods, when in doubt, are done in 1/3 of the time it would take on the stove or in the oven. For instance, a whole chicken takes around 20 minutes for each pound in the oven to cook. Under tension, it should take approximately 5 minutes for every pound. In this recipe, go with 4 minutes for each pound, in addition to 2 additional minutes. It turned out splendidly, and I sincerely don't think I required the extra 2 minutes.

Choosing the Right Time for Pressure Cooking?

There are factors to check when picking the ideal opportunity for pressure cooking, and here are few to remember.**Temperature:** The temperature of the food will have any kind of effect when choosing an opportunity to set for pressure cooking — the colder the food, the more extended the cooking time. Solidified foods will take longer than those at room temp. For instance, solidified chicken bosoms will take around 10 minutes of high weight, while defrosted chicken will just take about 6 minutes.**Pot in Pot cooking:** This is the place you are preparing food in its very own pot or holder inside the weight cooker pot. I love this style of cooking, making a few parts of a meal without a moment's delay. For instance, white rice cooked right in the inward pot will take less time than if you put it in its very own holder. I wouldn't fret a couple of additional minutes since I have had much better outcomes utilizing PIP cooking with rice than putting it legitimately in the inner pot of the Ninjaz Foody. I like to use aluminum cake container. They direct warmth well overall, so the expansion in time isn't so much as though you are using a weight safe earthenware holder. I will dig into PIP cooking more in a future article and welcome any inquiries you may have.**Nature of Food**: By far, this is the most significant thought while picking your weight cooking time. Remember, the thickness and size of the food, denser, and larger quantities of foods will take longer. For instance, an entire potato can take 10-15 minutes of weight cooking time sections. Little diced potatoes that take 1-2 minutes or a whole 3 lb. Hamburger dish will take longer than a 3 lb. Hamburger cook cut into lumps.

How much Liquid Can We Use When Pressure Cooking?

This is an uncontrollably discussed theme, and I am just imparting my insight dependent on various preliminaries and (fortunately few) blunders when cooking under tension. The fast answer is, it depends. I know that is not what you need to hear.Tragically, there isn't an accurate measure of fluid as long as your pot can come up to weight. Particular sorts of liquids are not reasonable for making steam required for pressure cooking and may cause a consume notice, for example, milk, cream-based soups, and tomato sauce. You can utilize these fluids.

However, you will likewise need to include a more slender fluid so your pot will come up to weight. It is the slight fluid that creates the steam required to cook under tension.Jambalaya Soup. When choosing the measure of fluid, remember what you need your final product to be. For instance, when making white rice, I generally utilize a 1:1 proportion of fluid to rice, if that is the main thing in the pot. At the point when I made this yummy Jambalaya Soup, I utilized 64 ounces of fluid (in addition to some from different sources). I don't need any additional liquid when making rice. However, I need my soup to be soup.Likewise, remember what fluid will be discharged or retained from the food you are cooking. For instance, a hamburger toss dish will deliver a lot of fluid all alone during the weight cooking process. In this way, for a delightful sauce, I may just include 1-2 cups of liquid with the understanding that I will wind up with around 3-4 cups. Would I be able to add 3 or 4 cups in any case? Indeed, yet I would wind up with a weakened tasting fluid not appropriate for the sauce.Pressure cooking grants a ton of flavor in a

short measure of time, so you can accomplish that cooked-throughout the day taste in a small amount of the time.**Fast Tip:** Use soups rather than water to upgrade the kind of your dishes truly.

Steam Function:

I love all the elements of the Ninjaz Foody and discover for every one of them, yet the steam work is my go-to while warming scraps that aren't air singed. I put what I need to re-heat into an aluminum cake dish spread with foil and put on the rack (high or low situation) with 2 cups of water in the base. I set the steam work for 5-10 minutes relying upon the thickness of the food I'm warming and Voila! Splendidly cooked food that holds its dampness without overcooking.The steam work is not the same as the weight cooking capacity as it enables steam to get away while cooking foods. This is an excellent alternative for veggies, sensitive fish, and rice. You can likewise expel the top during the steaming procedure to mind foods, yet be cautious and open it away from you because there is a ton of steam developed, and it's hot.I, as of late, made a moderate cooker (in the Ninjaz Foody) pork curry and chose to re-heat it simultaneously. I was making new rice. I utilized this bamboo steamer with the 6" Fat Daddio cake skillet, and it worked splendidly.

Slow Cook Function:

As though there weren't sufficient uses for the Ninjaz Foody, it even has a moderate cook work. You can as well set the temp to high or low and make sure to turn the dark valve to vent when controlled cooking. We need to discharge the developed steam. While the more excellent parts of us like the speed of pressure cooking, the average cook work sure has its employments. A day or two ago, I was attempting to choose what to make for supper and understood that the entirety of my meats was solidified. Of course, I could have pressure cooked hardened meat. However, it was promptly in the day, and I chose to evaluate pork tenderloin in the moderate cooker. I dumped in the ingredients, set the temperature on high, and my curry pork and veggies were done in time for supper. It was an indulgent sort of supper and incredibly yummy. I have heard few persons say that the moderate cook work on the Ninjaz Foody doesn't satisfy hopes dependent on remain solitary moderate cookers. What I discovered is that it takes significantly longer for the Ninjaz Foody to warm-up utilizing the flexible cook work. However, it surely carried out responsibility. I have just given it a shot high up until this point, and it truly cooked the pork tenderloin flawlessly.

Sear/Sauté Function:

I love this component of the Ninjaz Foody and use it constantly. Presently, you won't get that incredible singe on meats as you do in a treated steel pot, yet I locate the burn is adequate for what I am utilizing it for. The Ninjaz Kitchen is going to offer a hardened steel pot soon, and that is excessively energizing! You can utilize this setting on a few different temperatures, even though I will, in general, use the high setting the most. It is incredible for sautéing vegetables before including

stock and unusual ingredients to make soups or stews and warming the milk to make Homemade Yogurt in the Ninjaz Foody. I even utilized it to make the base for frozen yogurt a few evenings ago.

Air Crisp Function:

One of the most significant selling purposes of the Ninjaz Foody is the Air Crisp Function! It works extraordinary. Perhaps the best thing about the Ninjaz Foody is that you can pressure cook and afterward utilize the air fresh capacity to dark-colored the meat or fresh the top.To get directly to the point, I had my questions about air singing. That is the reason I never got one, yet I am certainly happy to have one at this point. Ninjaz Foody Recipe Asian Sticky Wings My first test was utilizing the air fresh mode on the Ninjaz Foody was making these Asian Sticky Wings. Gracious, man! They were so fresh and delightful, and I was sold on the Ninjaz Foody starting thereon.

Would it be a good idea for me to Use the Basket or Rack When Air Frying?

An inquiry I get a great deal is when to utilize the container stanzas the rack. I will go into significantly more profundity on this in a future article, yet I would like to address the subject genuine brisk.The bushel that accompanies the foody is intended to be utilized with the air fryer, prepare or steam work. Continuously use it with the diverter (those removable legs), so air can circle under the crate and help cook and dark-colored the base of the food.By the sheer structure of the container, it sits lower in the inward pot, so the food is further away from the warmth source. I have discovered that it takes more time to air fry utilizing the crate than the rack; in any case, there are times when that is something to be thankful for. For instance, if you are air searing a breaded bit of uncooked chicken bosom, having it in the bushel will permit the time required for the chicken to cook before the outside completes as well.Update: I utilized the crate to air fresh some cauliflower nibbles the previous evening, and the base browned up pleasantly. It was darker than the top. It was all the more a torment to clean; however, despite everything I figure, the rack makes a superior showing with uniformly air crisping.I utilize the rack all the more regularly when air fricasseeing because it permits progressively surface region of the food to be presented to the air crisping, and it cooks all the more equally as I would see it.

The drawback of the rack is you can just fit such a great amount on it. If you have the twofold rack, remember that foods on the base won't complete as fast, so you may need to pivot them. I constantly flip my food when air crisping to get the two sides pleasant and fresh.**Brisk tip:** If you have a food that you need to AC in the bushel, however, are stressed, it will stick. Cut around the state of the material the size of the container and jab a few openings in it to permit the air stream. At that point, place the round in the base of the bushel and spot food on top. It makes tidying up a breeze as well.

Bake/Roast Function:

The bake/roast work on the Ninjaz Foody works simply like a little convection oven. I completed a few tests with this capacity since individuals were stating that they were consuming their food when utilizing the prepare/broil work. What I discovered is that the temperatures are precise. At the point when you set it to 350° F, it warms up to 350° F. So, for what reason does it cook food quicker? As a result of the fan that courses the sight-seeing.When cooking in a convection oven, food completes faster. Now and then, this is incredible, and some of the time, as with bread and denser foods, it can leave you with food that is excessively darker outwardly and not cooked in the center. To alter for this, I propose diminishing the temperature by 50° F. For instance: if your cornbread recipe states to heat at 425° F, set the prepare/broil capacity to 375° F and cook for the expressed time. Keep in mind that you can generally lift the cover to check the advancement. Simply don't do it to an extreme, since you let out the warmth each time you open the top.

Broil Function:

I've had a couple of individuals inquire as to whether there is a contrast between the heat/cook work and the broil capacity. There is! It gets more sizzling than the heat/broil work by 25° F. While you can't set a temperature for the sear capacity, it will find a good pace 425º F following 15 minutes.I will plunge further into the utilizations for this capacity soon. I haven't had sufficient opportunity to do the testing on this yet.

Dehydration Function:

I have begun to look all starry eyed at this capacity without a doubt! The most entertaining thing is, I haven't utilized it yet for getting dried out. The drying out Homemade Yogurt in the Ninjaz Foody function enables you to set the Ninjaz Foody for very low temperatures that are extraordinary for sealing bread in a fraction of the time it takes on the counter. The other incredible news is you can make natively constructed yogurt utilizing the lack of hydration capacity and things being what they are, superb! On the off chance that you have not obtained a Ninjaz Foody yet, I energetically prescribe getting one with the parchedness work. I incline there will be a lot a greater number of employments for this capacity than simply drying out.

How can I Convert Instant Pot Recipes for The Ninjaz Foody?

This is an inquiry I see posed to a great deal, so I needed to take a couple of moments to address it. There aren't that numerous Ninjaz Foody explicit recipes out there because the apparatus is so new. It requires some investment to create, test, and compose a recipe that can be copied by any degree of the cook. I realize I'm constantly working on new methods, and I'd wager other food bloggers are, as well. Most Instant Pot recipes are composed utilizing the HIGH or LOW weight settings. They can be effectively changed over to the Ninjaz Foody's weight cooking capacity by adhering to similar instructions. On the off chance that a recipe doesn't state High or Low setting for pressure cooking, expect it is high. While there is a distinction in wattage between different models of weight cookers and the Ninjaz Foody, the wattage is just going to influence the time it takes to come up to weight. When any weight cooker comes up to pressure, it will arrive at a specific gravity for every square inch and keep up a similar temperature inside the pot. Remember, however, that it has been said all around the weight cooking world that each pot appears to cook a piece unexpectedly. There are numerous factors; elevation, the temperature of ingredients, size of food, and so forth, that can influence pressure cooking. Every individual has specific preferences, also. In this way, for one individual, pasta cooked for 10 minutes is excellent, and for another, it would be soft. If you realize you like your veggies fresh or your pasta still somewhat firm, consistently decline the cooking time by a couple of moments. You can generally include time, yet you can't un-cook food.

CHAPTER TWO SCRUMPTIOUS BREAKFAST DISHES FOR YOUR GRILL

Grilled Bacon-and-Herb Grit Cakes

Cooling the cornmeal encourages them to hold their shape and makes them sufficiently firm to cut when grilled.Ingredients

- 4 cups hot cooked instant cornmeal1/2 cup (2 ounces) destroyed white cheddar cheese1 tablespoon minced new or 1 teaspoon dried thyme2 teaspoons hacked crisp parsley1/2 teaspoon garlic powder1/2 teaspoon dark pepper3 bacon cuts, cooked and disintegratedCooking splash

The most effective method to make it

Consolidate the first seven ingredients in an enormous bowl; mix well. Empty the cornmeal into a 10-inch square baking dish covered with a cooking splash, spreading uniformly. Spread and chill for 1 hour or until totally crisp.Get ready, grill.Modify cornmeal onto a cutting board; cut into four squares. Cut each square corner to corner into two triangles.Spot corn meal triangles on grill rack covered with cooking splash; grill 5 minutes on each side or until delicately caramelized and wholly warmed.

Open-air fire Fried Eggs with Potato-and-Bacon Hash

Cook the quintessential outdoorsy breakfast: eggs and potato hash singed in bacon drippings. Mix a fresh pot of cattle rustler espresso straightforwardly over the pit fire to finish the meal.

Ingredients

- 1 pound child Yukon Gold potatoes8 ounces cut baconCoarse salt and newly ground pepperExtra-virgin olive oil8 huge eggs3 scallions, hacked

Directions

Cook potatoes in a massive pan of bubbling water until delicate, around 15 minutes.Cook bacon in a cast-iron skillet set over a pit fire or on a medium-high grill, turning once in a while, until fresh, around 10 minutes. Evacuate bacon, let cool marginally; disintegrate.Add potatoes to skillet, delicately crush each utilizing the rear of a spoon, and cook until only beginning to dark-colored, around 5 minutes. Season with salt and pepper. Mix disintegrated bacon into the skillet. Push hash to the other side of the skillet.Working in bunches, and including oil varying, split two eggs into the skillet, season with salt and pepper, and cook until wanted. Mix scallions into hash. Serve eggs with mixture.

Grilled Apricots with Brie, Prosciutto, and Honey

<u>A simple to make, sweet, salty, and delectable grilled starter! These Grilled Apricots with Brie, Prosciutto, and Honey are ideal for your next grill!</u>

Ingredients

- 5 apricots, divided4 cuts of prosciutto cut into thirds and folded up into chambers10 little wedges of brie cheese (around 2 ounces), room temperatureHoney for sprinkling on top

Instructions

Preheat grill to medium-high warmth.Brush the cut side of the divided apricots with a little oil or shower with cooking splash.Place the apricots chop side down on the grill and grill for a few minutes or until marginally mollified and grill marks are available.Place the apricots on a serving plate and promptly top with a cut of brie and moved up a bit of prosciutto.Drizzle the apricots with nectar and serve.

NotesBest served immediately as the more they sit, the more squeezes the apricots discharge.

Grilled French toast with Strawberries and Rosemary

Ingredients

- Vegetable oil, for brushing the grill1-quart strawberries, quartered2 tablespoons matured balsamic vinegarJuice of 1 orange, in addition to 2 teaspoons orange pizzazz1 sprig crisp rosemary3 eggs3/4 cup substantial cream2 tablespoons nectar1 teaspoon vanilla concentrateKosher saltSix 1-inch cuts challah breadPowdered sugar, for tidying, discretionary

Direction

Preheat a cast-iron grill skillet to medium and brush with oil. Spot the strawberries on an enormous bit of foil. Top with the balsamic, squeezed orange, get-up-and-go, and rosemary. Crease up the edges of the foil to shape a fixed parcel and spot on one corner of the grill. Cook until the strawberries are warmed through and relaxed, 3 to 5 minutes. In a shallow baking dish, join the eggs, cream, nectar, vanilla, and a spot of salt. Rush until consistently consolidated. Plunge the two sides of the bread cuts in the custard blend, and afterward move to the grill. Cook until the first side of the French toast is brilliant dark-colored, around 2 minutes. Tenderly flip and cook the opposite side, one more moment or two. Expel from the grill and move to a platter. Spoon the strawberries on top and residue with powdered sugar whenever wanted.

Grilled Breakfast Pizza
<u>Grill some pizza mixture, split three eggs on top, and include some bacon and cheese and presto! Grilled Breakfast Pizza.</u>

Ingredients

- 12 ounces, weight Prepared Pizza DoughOlive Oil, For Drizzling On Pizza Dough3 entire Eggs3 strips Cooked Bacon, Cut into Pieces1 cup Grated Mozzarella¼ cups Grated Parmesan1 squeeze Kosher Salt1 squeeze Freshly Cracked Pepper1 Tablespoon Minced Flat-leaf Parsley1 Tablespoon Minced Chives1 entire Scallion, Trimmed and Thinly Sliced

Instructions

Liberally dust the outside of your kitchen counter with flour and move pizza mixture to a 1/4-inch thickness. Sprinkle the two sides of the mix with olive oil and put aside on a plate. Assemble every one of the fixings and batter and move outside beside the grill. When your grill is decent and hot, place the pizza mixture on the most sweltering piece of the grill, making a point to check it at regular intervals or so to guarantee appropriate cooking. When grill marks show up, flip it and move the mixture to a spot on the grill that doesn't have direct warmth. Split the three eggs onto the batter and spread for 2-3 minutes. When the eggs are about to be set, sprinkle the cheeses, bacon and salt and pepper. Spread for an extra 1-2 minutes, or until cheese is softened. Move instantly to a plate and sprinkle with parsley, chives, and scallions. Note: If you're not in the state of mind to start up the grill, at that point, here's the best approach to cook it in the oven. My recommendation is to get yourself a "pizza stone" from Lowes or Home Depot. Pre-heat your oven to 450F, reveal the batter, split the eggs on top, sprinkle with mozzarella and parmesan cheese, at that point include the bits of bacon and salt and pepper. Cook in the oven for 8 to 12 minutes, keeping an eye on it following 5 minutes and pivoting it if fundamental. At the point when the outside layer is brilliant, the cheese is softened, and the eggs yolks are cooked to medium expel from the oven.

Grilled bruschetta portobello mushrooms

Grilled Bruschetta Portobello Mushrooms covered in garlic margarine are your new most loved approach to eat a mushroom! Breakfast, Lunch, OR supper!

Ingredients

- 2 cups grape or cherry tomatoes, divided3 tablespoons red onion finely cleaved3 tablespoons crisp basil destroyed, separatedSalt and pepper to taste4 tablespoons Garlic Butter1 teaspoon dried oregano6 enormous Portobello Mushrooms stem expelled, washed and dried altogether with a paper towelBalsamic Glaze: (or you can utilize locally acquired, or this recipe)1/4 cup balsamic vinegar2 teaspoons darker sugar OPTIONAL

Instructions

Preheat grill plates, a grill skillet, or a bar-b-que on medium warmth. Softly oil grill plates with cooking oil.Combine the red onion, tomatoes, 2 tablespoons of the crisp basil, salt, and pepper in a medium-sized bowl. Blend until very much consolidated. Put in a safe spot.Combine the Garlic Butter and oregano in a little pan (or microwave-safe bowl), and soften until garlic is fragrant. Brush each mushroom with garlic spread on all sides.Grill for 5 minutes, until only starting to relax.At the point when mushrooms are done, top with the tomato/basil blend, and shower with the balsamic coating. Sprinkle with some additional salt, to your preferences, and enhancement with the remixing basil leaves to serve.

For the Balsamic Glaze:

(In the case of making without any preparation, get ready while mushrooms are grilling.) Combine sugar (if utilizing) and vinegar in a little pot over high warmth and bring to the bubble. Diminish warmth to low; permit to stew for 5-8 minutes or until blend has thickened and decreased to a coating. (If not utilizing sugar, permit to diminish for 12-15 minutes on low warmth.)

For The Oven:

Preheat oven to grill/sear settings on high heat. Mastermind oven rack to the center of your oven. Follow the directions above to set up your mushrooms with the garlic margarine. Spot them, buttered side down, on a baking plate. Grill/sear until for around 8 minutes until mushrooms start to darken.When cooked, proceed with the directions above.

Notes

To dry portobellos, ensure you utilize a dry piece of paper towel per mushroom and daintily press sheet into each mushroom to delicately crush out the overabundance fluid. If this step isn't done thoroughly, the portobellos will discharge a great deal of fluid during cook time.

Avocado Eggs on the Grill

We see more breakfast recipes increasingly with the avocado and egg combo, and this recipe makes it conceivable to appreciate the two together, grilled. The avocado is given an additional portion of flavor from grill flavoring and afterward fills in as a defensive, and tasty, shell for the egg to cook in.

Ingredients

- 1 ready avocadopinch of grill rub2 eggsSalt and pepper, to taste1 red jalapeño, finely diced (discretionary)1 tomato, cleaved

Directions

Preheat the grill to 500 degrees.Run a blade cutting edge around the boundary of the pit of the avocado the long way and expel the hole. Scoop out enough of the green substance to account for an egg. Coat within every avocado with a spot of the grill flavoring. Break an egg into every half.Spot the avocado parts on the grill for around 5 minutes, or until the egg whites are firm and the yolk is as yet runny. Expel from the grill, plate, and top with a bit of flavoring, diced pepper, and tomato.

Eggs Benedict Burger

Firm bacon, a poached egg, and hollandaise sauce top this supper meets-breakfast burger.

Ingredients

For the hollandaise sauce:

- 3 huge egg yolks1 Tbsp water1 stick unsalted spread, cut into 8 piecesJuice from 1/2 a lemonSaltPepper

For the burgers

- 1 lb. lean ground meatSaltPepperWorcestershire3 eggs, seared or poached3 cuts of bacon, cooked to a freshEnglish biscuits or burger buns

Instructions

Heat grill to medium-high warmth.In a heatproof plate set over a skillet of stewing water, whisk egg yolks with water, whisking energetically, until blend thickens, around 5 minutes.Remove from warmth, and mix in lemon juice.Whisk in 1-2 bits of margarine at once until softened.Season with salt and pepper. Keep warm over the double heater, whisking sporadically, and including 1-2 tsp boiling water if the sauce thickens excessively.Season ground hamburger with a touch of salt, dark pepper, and a couple of runs of Worcestershire.Divide ground hamburger into three equivalent bits and structure into a patty.Cook on grill about 5 minutes each side until cooked to wanted doneness.Assemble on buns and top with fresh bacon, an egg, and a spoonful of hollandaise sauce.

Yields: 3 servings**Assessed time:** 30 minutes

Shakshuka
A delectable Middle Eastern egg dish made on the stovetop. Vegetarian, gluten-free, sound, and delicious.

Ingredients

- 1 tbsp olive oil1/2 onion, stripped and diced1 clove garlic, minced1 chime pepper, seeded and hacked4 cups ready diced tomatoes, or 2 jars (14 oz. each) diced tomatoes2 tbsp tomato glue1 tsp gentle stew powder1 tsp of cumin1 tsp of paprikaPinch of cayenne pepper to taste (cautious, it's hot!)Pinch of sugar (discretionary, to taste - exclude for low carb)Salt and pepper, to taste6 eggs1/2 tbsp new hacked parsley (discretionary, for decorate)

Instructions

Heat a deep, enormous skillet or sauté container on medium. Gradually warm olive oil in the skillet. Include slashed onion, sauté for a couple of moments until the onion starts to mellow. Add garlic and keep on sauté till blend is fragrant.Add the diced chile pepper, sauté for 5-7 minutes over medium until mollified.Add tomatoes and tomato glue to the dish, mix until mixed. Include flavors and sugar, mix, and enable blend to stew over medium warmth for 5-7 minutes until it begins to decrease.You can now taste the mixture and flavor it as indicated by your inclinations. Add pepper and salt to taste, more sugar for a better sauce or more cayenne pepper for a spicier shakshuka (be cautious with the cayenne, it is very fiery!).Crack the eggs, each in turn, straightforwardly over the tomato blend, making a point to space them equally over the sauce. I generally place 5 eggs around the external edge and 1 on the inside. The eggs will cook "over simple" style over the tomato sauce.Cover the dish. Enable blend to stew for 10-15 minutes, or until the eggs are cooked, and the sauce has marginally decreased. Watch out for the skillet to ensure that the sauce doesn't diminish excessively, which can prompt consuming.Some individuals lean toward their shakshuka eggs progressively runny. If this is your inclination, let the sauce decrease for a couple of moments before breaking the eggs on top- - at that point, spread the skillet and cook the eggs to taste. Enhancement with the cleaved parsley, whenever wanted.Shakshuka can be had for breakfast, lunch, or supper. For breakfast, present with warm, dry bread or pita that can be dunked into the sauce (on the off chance that you are gluten-bigoted or observing Passover, skirt the food). For supper, present with a greenside serving of mixed greens for a light, simple meal.

Grilled Fried Eggs
<u>Keep the kitchen cool by getting ready singed eggs on the grill in singular smaller than usual foil plate. It's a fun presentation, and cleanup is simple!</u>

Ingredients
- Aluminum foilVegetable oil or cooking splashEggsPepper

Instruction

Preheat grill to medium warmth (about 350°F/180°C).For each egg, make a little round plate or vessel with aluminum foil. To do this, overlap a bit of foil (around 5 x 12 inches/13 x 30 cm) into equal parts. Shape the double thickness of foil into a round plate, around 4 inches (10 cm) in breadth, by bending up the edge to frame a lip, at that point collapsing over as vital.Brush the bottoms of the plate with oil or coat with cooking splash. Spot the plate on the grill. Split an egg into every dish.Close the top and cook for two or three minutes until egg whites begin to set. For a delicate yolk, open the lid and keep cooking for 2 to 3 minutes until eggs are cooked as wanted. For a firm yolk, complete the process of preparing with the top shut.Remove from grill. Sprinkle with pepper.

Tips:

- To fill the plate effectively, split each egg into a little cup first. At that point, fill the dish.To cook an over-simple egg, cause a marginally more significant plate so you too can without much of a stretch slip a flipper under the egg to turn it over when the white of the egg sets. Grill the second side for about a moment.To make a two-egg serving, make a bigger oval-molded foil plate.To grill more eggs one after another, utilization an enormous bit of foil with the edge bent up. Brush foil with oil or coat with a cooking splash, set the foil over the grill, at that point, break eggs on top. If the grill is marginally inclined, when each egg is put on the foil, hold it set up quickly with a flipper until it sets.

- Serve eggs with toast or with a cut of cheese in a grilled burger bun.

Omelet on the Grill

Make an omelet on the grill and include that Smokey, BBQ flavor to your breakfast.

Ingredients

- 2 eggs1 tablespoon milk½ cup destroyed cheese (whichever type you like)1 cut bacon (extra pieces are discretionary for a side dish)Salt and pepper to taste

Instructions

Heat the grill to medium warmthAdd bacon to grill and cook until fresh, around 3-4 each sideRemove bacon and spot-on paper towelGrab a 9" pie plate and spread the base with tin foilCoat within the plate with nonstick cooking splashIn a different bowl, whisk together eggs, milk, cheese, and salt and pepperAdd the blend to pie plate and spot on the grillClose cover and cook 3-4 minutesWhen the center of the omelet starts to lift, and the eggs start taking a strong structure, disintegrate one bit of bacon and add to half of the omeletLift the bacon-less side of the omelet with a spatula and crease over the side you just added the bacon toClose the cover and then cook for 2 minutesFlip the whole omelet over and let cook until the eggs are never again runny (around 2-3 minutes)Remove from grill and serve warmDig in!

Grilled Breakfast Casserole

<u>A flavorful, simple breakfast meal to nourish a group. Simple to make on the BBQ grill!</u>

Ingredients

- 500 grams solidified hash brown or potato tots8 eggs3/4 cup milk1 bundle chicken frankfurter interfaces, cooked and cleaved (or other sausages, bacon or ham)1 medium onion, hacked1 red chile pepper, slashed1 cup new mushrooms, slashedSeasoning salt and pepper to taste1 cup destroyed cheese

Instructions

Heat bar-b-que grill to 350 degrees (ish)Spray the base of an expendable aluminum foil lasagna skillet with cooking splash.Press the hash browns or potato tots into the base (helps if they are defrosted).Mix the eggs and milk in a medium bowl.Layer sausage, onion, bell pepper, and mushrooms onto the potatoes.Pour the egg blend over everything.Season with salt and pepper.Sprinkle the top with destroyed cheese.Cover dish with aluminum foil and spot on the preheated grill.Cook for 30 minutes or until eggs are set. Expel foil for the last 5-10 minutes so that the cheese will make dark-colored.

Grilled Hash Browns
Ingredients

- 3-1/2 cups solidified cubed hash dark-colored potatoes, defrosted1 little onion, cleaved1 tablespoon meat bouillon granulesDash prepared saltDash pepper1 tablespoon spread, liquefied

Directions

Place potatoes on a bit of uncompromising foil (around 20 in. x 18 in.) covered with cooking splash. Sprinkle with onion, bouillon, prepared salt, and pepper; shower with the spread.Fold foil around potatoes and seal firmly. Grill, secured, over circuitous medium warmth for 10-15 minutes or until potatoes are delicate, turning once.

Campfire French Toast
Ingredients

- 1 portion of the bread of decision8 eggs¼ cup milk1 tsp vanilla1 tsp cinnamon¼ cup cut almonds1 500g compartment of new strawberriesConfectioners' sugar (Icing Sugar)Syrup of decision

Instructions

Wash strawberries, dice half of the compartment, and cut the other half.Wrap the portion of bread in the material paper, at that point in foil freely, so the bread cuts fall marginally open.Sprinkle the diced strawberries over the portion, taking consideration to sprinkle some between cuts; put in a safe spot the cut strawberries for a short time later.Sprinkle the cut almonds similarly as the diced strawberries over the portion.Whisk eggs, milk, vanilla, and cinnamon until foamy. Wrap the foil and material paper more tightly around the part of the bread. Pour eggs equally over the whole portion of bread before wrapping firmly with a top bit of foil to guarantee no breaks.Place over the pit fire or grill on low to medium warmth for roughly 40 minutes, moving around every so often to cook equally. On the off chance that the bread looks saturated still, cook somewhat more.Remove from warmth and let sit for 10 mins before presenting with sugar, syrup, and cut strawberries.

Coconut French Toast with Grilled Pineapple

Ingredients

- 1 cup light coconut milk1/4 cup sugar1/4 cup without fat milk3 huge eggs1 (12-ounce) portion French bread, cut into 15 cutsCooking splash10 (1/4-inch-thick) cuts stripped pineapple1/2 cup chipped improved coconut

Instructions

Preheat oven to 200°. Spot a baking sheet in the oven.Consolidate coconut milk, sugar, sans fat milk, and eggs in a shallow dish, blending with a whisk. Working in clusters, plunge bread in the milk blend, and let represent 1 moment on each side.Heat a huge nonstick skillet over medium-high warmth, and coat container with cooking shower. Add 5 covered bread cuts to the dish, and cook for 2 minutes on each side or until seared. Spot on a warm skillet in the oven to keep warm. Rehash strategy in bunches with cooking shower, remaining cuts, and milk blend.Heat a grill container over medium-high warmth. Include pineapple and grill for 2 minutes on each side or until well-stamped. Cleave pineapple. Spot 3 cuts of French toast on every one of 5 plates, and partition the pineapple among servings. Top with coconut.

Grilled Sausages

Ingredients

- 16 wiener joins (pork or chicken, sweet or hot, or a blend)Crusty bread or rolls (discretionary)

Instructions

Heat grill. Prick every meat in a few spots with a fork. Spot the frankfurters legitimately on the mesh and grill, infrequently turning, until cooked through, 10 to 15 minutes. (The frankfurters can be cooked on any piece of the grill, any place space permits. But if they're not over direct warmth, cook a couple of moments longer.) If wanted, serve on the dried-up bread or rolls.

Grilled Fruit Packets

Grilled Fruit Packets will fulfill even the most significant sweet tooth—for significantly fewer calories. This organic product pastry is perfect for sweltering days when baking is an excessive amount to tolerate. Consider serving the natural product on grilled pound cake, whenever wanted.

Ingredients

- 3 bananas, cut 3/4-inch thick1 pound strawberries, stemmed and split3 oranges, stripped, cut into portions1/2 pineapple, peeled, cored, cut into 1-inch pieces1/4 cup stuffed light dark colored sugar1 teaspoon cinnamon16 entire cloves4 tablespoons unsalted butter1/4 cup rum, discretionary

Instructions

Spread out eight 12-by-12-inch bits of uncompromising foil on a ledge. Gap organic product equally among foil pieces, setting it on the base portion of foil pieces. Combine sugar and cinnamon. Put two cloves on each square and sprinkle with sugar blend. Dab each with 1/2 Tbsp. Margarine and 1/2 Tbsp. Rum, whenever wanted. Crease top portion of foil over foods grown from the ground edges to seal.Preheat grill to low. Spot bundles on grill and cook for 10 minutes. Expel from warmth and let cool for 5 minutes. Cautiously open bundles, fill bowls and present with frozen yogurt or whipped cream, whenever wanted.

Grilled French toast Kebabs

Thirty minutes, in addition to overnight for the portion to stand. Three stunts for immaculate outcomes: Use day-old bread, slice each solid bread shape to incorporate some outside, and splash the sticks.

Ingredients

- 1 portion (1 lb.) day-old torment a lev in3/4 cup entire milk4 huge eggs1 teaspoon vanilla concentrateMelted spreadMaple or berry syrupPowdered sugar (discretionary)

The most effective method to make it

Drench 12 wooden sticks (10 to 12 in.) in water to cover for 20 minutes; channel. In the interim, heat a grill to medium (350°).Cut enough bread into 1-in. Pieces, remembering some covering for each, to make 2 quantities; additional extra for different employments.Whisk milk, eggs, and vanilla in a huge bowl to mix. Blend in bread to cover, at that point string onto sticks.Oil cooking grate, utilizing tongs and an oiled wad of paper towels. Grill skewers, secured until baked, turning once, 3 to 4 minutes.Present with spread and syrup and residue with powdered sugar on the off chance that you like.Note: Nutritional investigation is per serving.

Farmhouse Breakfast

A farmhouse breakfast is best made as our forefathers would have done it, with bacon sung in an overwhelming skillet and eggs cooked in the brilliant drippings.

Ingredients

- 8 enormous eggsButter4 cuts hard bread, each around 1 inch thick8 thick cuts bacon1/4 teaspoon fit salt1/4 teaspoon ground dark pepper1 garlic clove, cut down the middle or jam

Step by step instructions to make it

Set up the grill for direct cooking over medium warmth (350° to 450°F).Split every one of the eggs delicately into a considerable bowl. Spread the bread cuts on the two sides.Brush the cooking grates clean. Mastermind the bacon in a solitary layer in a 12-inch cast-iron skillet, with pieces on the base and around the sides. Grill over direct medium warmth, with the top shut however much as could be expected, until fresh, 15 to 20 minutes, turning and modifying the bacon as it cooks and psychologists. Channel the bacon on paper towels and afterward envelop by foil and keep warm on the grill's warming rack or in a low oven.Utilize a large serving spoon to scoop out about a portion of the bacon oil from the skillet, leaving a ⅛-inch layer on the base. Tenderly empty every one of the eggs into the skillet without a moment's delay and season with the salt and pepper. Spot the bread straightforwardly on the grill and cook both the eggs and the bread over direct medium warmth, with the cover shut however much as could be expected, until the eggs start to cover over on top (the yolks will be somewhat runny) and bread is toasted. The eggs will take about 6 minutes, and the toast will take 3 to 4 minutes. Turn the dough once during grilling. Move the toast to the warming rack or oven with the bacon.Utilizing a serving spoon or spatula, cut the eggs separated and scoop them out of the skillet each in turn. But if the savory toast is wanted, rub each side with the cut side of the garlic clove while the toast is still warm. If sweet toast is liked, spread it with jam. Serve the eggs and toast promptly with the bacon.

Plum-Glazed Sausage

Offer Bratwurst, Bockwurst, and weisswurst with new chicken or hot pork sausage.Ingredients

- 3/4 cup plum protects2 tablespoons balsamic vinegar2 teaspoons cleaved crisp thyme1/4 teaspoon crisply ground pepper2 pounds grouped crisp hotdogs

Step by step instructions

Preheat grill to 305° to 350° (medium) heat. Cook first 4 ingredients in a little pan over low warmth, frequently blending, 5 minutes; hold half of the blend.Grill sausages, secured with a grill cover, 10 to 12 minutes or until done, turning once in a while and brushing with staying half of plum blend during most recent 5 minutes of grilling. Expel from heat; let stand 5 minutes. Present with the held plum blend.

Grilled Peaches with Honey

If you've never encountered the enjoyment of grilled peaches, you're painfully passing up a significant opportunity.

Ingredients

- 3 peaches, pitted and split1 tablespoon olive oil1 tablespoon nectar

The most effective method to make it

Preheat grill to high.Cut peaches down the middle; expel pits.Brush cut side of peach parts with olive oil and spot on grill, chops side down.Grill until brilliant dark colored and caramelized, 2 to 3 minutes.Turn peach parts over and grill until somewhat delicate and simply warmed through, around 2 minutes longer.Expel from grill and shower with nectar.

Grilled Breakfast Burrito

Ingredients

- 1/4cup vegetable oil2large potatoes, diced1onion, diced
- 1/2bell pepper, diced1/4cup spread or 1/4 cup margarine8eggs, beaten1lb breakfast hotdog or 1 lb. chorizo sausage, cooked and depleted1teaspoon salt1/2teaspoon new ground dark pepper1cup Monterey jack cheese, destroyed1cup sharp cheddar cheese, destroyed10large flour tortillasNonstick cooking splash

Directions

Heat up the 1/4 cup of oil in a large skillet over medium warmth. Fry potatoes until nearly cooked through, at that point, include onions and peppers, proceeding to cook until vegetables are delicate. Drain put in a safe spot.In a similar skillet, dissolve spread or margarine over medium warmth. Scramble eggs, including potatoes, vegetables, and hotdog during the last couple of seconds of cooking. Add salt and pepper to taste.Top every tortilla with cheese and part of the egg blend, fold into a burrito. Splash a hot grill (I utilize a family size George Foreman) with a cooking shower. Grill for about 11 minutes or until lightly brown.Serve hot with custom made Pico De Gallo, salsa, sharp cream, or maybe Spanish rice and refried beans.

CHAPTER THREE GRILLED RECIPES FOR DINNER

Steak Fajitas

Lively salsa and delicate portions of steak make these conventional fajitas additional exceptional.

Ingredients

- 2 enormous tomatoes, seeded and hacked1/2 cup diced red onion1/4 cup lime juice1 jalapeno pepper, seeded and minced3 tablespoons minced crisp cilantro2 teaspoons ground cumin, isolated3/4 teaspoon salt, isolated1 hamburger flank steak (around 1-1/2 pounds)1 tablespoon canola oil1 enormous onion, divided and cut6 entire wheat tortillas (8 inches), warmedOptional: Sliced avocado and lime wedges

Directions

For salsa, place the first 5 ingredients in a little bowl; mix in 1 teaspoon cumin and 1/4 teaspoon salt. Let remain until serving.Sprinkle steak with the rest of the cumin and salt. Grill, secured, over medium warmth, or cook 4 in. From heat until meat arrives at desired doneness (for medium-uncommon, a thermometer should peruse 135°), 6-8 minutes. Let stand for 5 minutes.Meanwhile, in a skillet, heat oil over medium-high warmth; sauté onion until fresh delicate. Cut steak daintily over the grain; serve in tortillas with onion and salsa. Whenever wanted, present with avocado and lime wedges.

Grilled Shrimp and Tomatoes with Linguine

Ingredients

- 8 ounces uncooked linguine16 cherry tomatoes2 tablespoons olive oil1 pound uncooked huge shrimp, stripped and deveined1/2 teaspoon pepper1/4 teaspoon salt1/4 teaspoon garlic powder1/4 teaspoon Italian flavoring2 tablespoons spread1/4 cup ground Parmesan cheese2 tablespoons torn new basil

Directions

In a huge pan, cook linguine as per bundle directions. In the interim, string tomatoes onto metal or splashed wooden sticks; brush with 1 tablespoon oil. String shrimp onto sticks; brush with residual fat. Blend seasonings; sprinkle over shrimp.Grill shrimp, secured, over medium warmth 3-4 minutes on each side or until shrimp turn pink. Grill tomatoes, secured, over medium heat 2-3 minutes or until somewhat relaxed, turning every so often.Drain linguine, saving 1/4 cup pasta water. In the same pot, liquefy margarine over medium warmth. Include linguine, cheese, and saved pasta water, hurling to join. Expel shrimp and tomatoes from sticks; present with pasta. Sprinkle with basil.

Chili Rubbed Ribs

Ingredients

- 3 tablespoons stuffed dark colored sugar2 tablespoons paprika2 tablespoons stew powder3 teaspoons ground cumin2 teaspoons garlic powder1 teaspoon salt6 pounds pork child back ribs

Glaze:

- 1 cup decreased sodium soy sauce1 cup stuffed dark colored sugar2/3 cup ketchup1/3 cup lemon juice1-1/2 teaspoons minced crisp gingerroot

Directions

Mix the first 6 ingredients; rub over ribs. Refrigerate, secured, 30 minutes.Wrap rib racks in enormous bits of rock-solid foil; seal firmly. Grill, covered, over indirect medium heat until tender, 1 to 1-1/2 hours.In a large pan, join coat ingredients; cook, revealed, over medium warmth until warmed through, and sugar is broken up, 6-8 minutes, blending every so often.Carefully expel ribs from foil. Spot ribs over direct warmth; brush with a portion of the coating. Grill, covered, over medium heat until cooked, 25-30 minutes, turning and brushing ribs occasionally with remaining glaze.

Test Kitchen Tips

- Balsamic vinegar is produced using sweet white grapes and gets its dim shading from maturing in wooden barrels. The more it ages, the more thick and soft it becomes. Profoundly developed kinds of vinegar are costly and best delighted in sprinkled over cheese or utilized for plunging with oil and bread. Reasonably valued vinegar works fine for planning sauces and decreases. If necessary, add a little sugar to taste.Avocado is high in monounsaturated fat, a purported "decent fat" that can bring down your blood cholesterol alongside the danger of stroke and coronary illness. Each natural product additionally contains around 9 grams of solid fiber.

Attempt these 30 salad recipes prepared in a short time.

Grilled Garden Veggie Pizza

Ingredients
- 1 small red onion, cut across into 1/2-inch cuts1 substantial sweet red pepper, divided, stemmed and seeded1 little zucchini, cut the long way into 1/2-inch cuts1 yellow summer squash cut the long way into 1/2-inch cuts2 tablespoons olive oil1/2 teaspoon salt1/4 teaspoon pepper1 prebaked 12-inch slender entire wheat pizza outside layer3 tablespoons jolted simmered minced garlic2 cups destroyed part-skim mozzarella cheese, partitioned1/3 cup torn new basil

Directions
Brush the vegetables with oil, then sprinkle with salt and pepper. Grill, covered, over medium heat until delicate, 4-5 minutes for each side for onion and pepper, 3-4 minutes for every side for zucchini and squash.Separate onion into rings; cut pepper into strips. Spread pizza outside layer with garlic; sprinkle with 1 cup cheese. Top with grilled vegetables, at that point remaining cheese.Grill pizza, secured, over medium warmth until the base is brilliant darker and cheese is liquefied 5-7 minutes. Top with basil.

Firecracker Grilled Salmon
Ingredients
- 2 tablespoons balsamic vinegar2 tablespoons diminished sodium soy sauce1 green onion, meagerly cut1 tablespoon olive oil1 tablespoon maple syrup2 garlic cloves, minced1 teaspoon ground ginger1 teaspoon squashed red pepper drops1/2 teaspoon sesame oil1/4 teaspoon salt4 salmon filets (6 ounces each)

Directions
In a little bowl, join the first 10 ingredients. Pour 1/4 cup marinade into an enormous resealable plastic pack. Include the salmon; seal the box, and go to cover. Refrigerate for as long as 30 minutes. Cover and refrigerate remaining marinade.Drain salmon, disposing of the marinade in the sack. Spot salmon skin side down on a lubed grill rack. Grill, secured, over high warmth or sear 3-4 in. From the

heat for 5-10 minutes or until fish drops effectively with a fork, treating every so often with outstanding marinade.

Steak and New Potato Toss
Ingredients

- 1 pound little red potatoes, cut into 1-inch wedges1 hamburger top sirloin steak (1 inch thick and around 1-1/4 pounds)3 cups crisp broccoli florets1/4 cup olive oil2 tablespoons juice vinegar2 garlic cloves, minced1/2 teaspoon ground mustard1/2 teaspoon paprika1/4 teaspoon pepper2 green onions, meagerly cut1 medium sweet red pepper, cleaved

Directions

Place potatoes in an enormous pot; add water to cover. Heat to the point of boiling. Decrease heat; cook, revealed, 10-15 minutes or until delicate. Drain.Meanwhile, grill steak, secured, over medium warmth 7-9 minutes on each side or until meat arrives at desired doneness (for medium-uncommon, a thermometer should peruse 135°; medium, 140°; medium-well, 145°).In a huge pan, place steamer bushel more than 1 in. Of water. Spot broccoli in the container. Heat water to the point of boiling. Diminish warmth to keep up a low bubble; steam, secured, 2-3 minutes or until broccoli is fresh delicate. Expel from heat.In a little bowl, whisk oil, vinegar, garlic, and seasonings until mixed; mix in green onions. Cut steak into tender cuts.In a considerable container, join potatoes, steak, broccoli, and red pepper. Sprinkle with vinaigrette; hurl to join. Serve warm or refrigerate and serve cold.

Grilled Pork Noodle Salad

The main complicated thing about this simple salad is the flavor! With smoky grilled pork and an assortment of new herbs and vegetables, this is a soothing and delectable home-prepared meal.

Ingredients

- 1 jalapeno pepper, seeded and minced3 tablespoons lime juice2 tablespoons fish sauce or soy sauce2 teaspoons darker sugar2 pork tenderloins (3/4 pound each), cut into 1/2-inch cuts1 bundle (8.8 ounces) vermicelli-style meager rice noodles

DRESSING:

- 1/4 cup water2 tablespoons lime juice1 tablespoon fish sauce or soy sauce1/2 teaspoon dark colored sugar

SALAD:

- 2 cups destroyed lettuce2 plum tomatoes, cut1 medium cucumber, julienned2 medium carrots, julienned1/2 cup coarsely hacked crisp cilantro1/4 cup approximately pressed new mint leaves

Directions

In a substantial resealable plastic pack, consolidate jalapeno, lime juice, fish sauce, and darker sugar. Include pork; seal sack and go to cover. Refrigerate 3 hours or medium-term.Drain pork, disposing of the marinade. Saturate a paper towel with cooking oil; utilizing since quite a while ago took care of tongs, rub on grill rack to cover daintily. Grill pork, secured, over medium warmth 1-2 minutes on each side or until a thermometer peruses 145°.Cook rice noodles as indicated by bundle directions. Channel and wash in chilly water; channel thoroughly. In a little bowl, whisk dressing ingredients. Separation rice noodles among six serving dishes. Organize vegetables, pork, and herbs over noodles; sprinkle with dressing and hurl to join.Wear dispensable gloves when cutting hot peppers; the oils can consume the skin. Abstain from contacting your face.

Chicken with Peach-Cucumber Salsa
Ingredients

- 1-1/2 cups hacked stripped new peaches (around 2 medium)3/4 cup hacked cucumber4 tablespoons peach jelly, divided3 tablespoons finely chopped red onion1 teaspoon minced fresh mint3/4 teaspoon salt, divided4 boneless skinless chicken bosom parts (6 ounces each)1/4 teaspoon pepper

Directions

For salsa, in a little bowl, consolidate peaches, cucumber, 2 tablespoons jelly, onion, mint, and 1/4 teaspoon salt.Sprinkle chicken with pepper and staying salt. On a softly lubed grill rack, grill chicken, secured, over medium warmth 5 minutes. Turn; grill 7-9 minutes longer or until a thermometer peruses 165°, brushing tops every so often with residual jam. Present with salsa.

Meat and Potato Kabobs
Ingredients

- 1 pound meat top sirloin steak, cut into 1-inch 3D shapes1-1/2 teaspoons steak flavoring, separated1 garlic clove, minced1 cup cola3 little red potatoes (around 8 ounces), cubed1 tablespoon water1 cup cherry tomatoes1 medium sweet orange pepper, cut into 1-inch pieces1 teaspoon canola oil1 cup pineapple chunks

Directions

Sprinkle hamburger with 1 teaspoon steak flavoring and garlic. Spot cola in an enormous bowl. Include meat; hurl to cover. Put in a safe spot.Place potatoes and water in a microwave-safe bowl. Microwave, covered, on high for 4-5 minutes or just until delicate; drain. Come back to the pan. Include tomatoes, pepper, oil, and remaining steak flavoring; delicately hurl to cover.Drain meat, disposing of the marinade. On eight metal or drenched wooden sticks, on the other hand, string hamburger, vegetables, and pineapple. Grill, covered, over medium heat, or cook 4 in. From heat 6-8 minutes or until meat arrives at desired doneness and pepper is fresh delicate, turning infrequently.

Garden Fish Tacos

Ingredients
- 1 medium ear sweet corn, husk expelled1 poblano pepper, split and seeds evacuated4 tilapia fillets (4 ounces each)1/8 teaspoon salt1 yellow summer squash, split the long way1 medium treasure tomato, slashed1/3 cup hacked red onion3 tablespoons coarsely hacked crisp cilantro1 teaspoon ground lime zest3 tablespoons lime juice8 taco shells, warmed1/2 medium ready avocado, peeled and cut

Directions
Lightly oil the grill rack. Grill corn and pepper, secured, over medium warmth 10-12 minutes or until delicate, turning once in a while. Cool marginally.Meanwhile, sprinkle fish with salt. Grill fish and squash, secured, over medium warmth 7-9 minutes or until fish just starts to drop effectively with a fork and squash is delicate, turning once.Cut the corn from cob and spot in a bowl. Slash pepper and squash; add to corn. Mix in tomato, onion, cilantro, lime zest, and lime juice. Serve fish in taco shells; top with corn blend and avocado cuts.

Steak with Chipotle-Lime Chimichurri

Steak gets a flavor kick from chimichurri. This delightful, universally handy herb sauce is so flexible, it supplements almost any grilled meat, poultry, or fish.

Ingredients
- 2 cups crisp parsley leaves1-1/2 cups fresh cilantro leaves1/2 medium red onion, coarsely slashed1 to 2 chipotle peppers5 garlic cloves, sliced1/2 cup of olive oil1/4 cup of white wine vinegar1 teaspoon ground lime zest

- 1/4 cup lime juice3 teaspoons dried oregano1-1/4 teaspoons salt, partitioned3/4 teaspoon pepper, partitioned2 pounds hamburger level iron steaks or 2 meat top sirloin steaks (1 pound each)

Directions

For the chimichurri, place the first 5 ingredients in a food processor; beat until finely cleaved. Include oil, vinegar, lime zest, lime juice, oregano, 1/2 teaspoon salt, and 1/4 teaspoon pepper; process until mixed. Move to a bowl; refrigerate, secured, until serving.Sprinkle steaks with the staying salt and pepper. Grill, achieved, over medium heat 5-8 minutes on each side or until meat arrives at desired doneness (for medium-uncommon, a thermometer should peruse 135°; medium, 140°; medium-well, 145°). Let stand 5 minutes before cutting. Present with chimichurri.

Rosemary-Lemon Grilled Chicken

Ingredients

- 1 medium lemon1/3 cup spread, cubed4 teaspoons minced new rosemary or 1 teaspoon dried rosemary, squashed2 garlic cloves, minced1/4 teaspoon salt1/4 teaspoon pepper4 boneless chicken breast halves (6 ounces each)

Directions

Finely grind strip from lemon and juice lemon. In a microwave, liquefy spread. Mix in lemon squeeze and piece, rosemary, garlic, salt, and pepper.Grill chicken, secured, over medium warmth or sear 4 in. From heat 5-7 minutes on each side or until a thermometer peruses 165°, often treating with margarine blend during the most recent 5 minutes of cooking.

Beef and Blue Cheese Penne with Pesto

Extraordinary and easy to set up, this heavenly pasta dish is loaded up with new flavors, and it's as sound as it is healthy. The best part is that there's nothing more needed than 30 minutes to set this meal on the table.

Ingredients

- 2 cups uncooked entire wheat penne pasta2 meat tenderloin steaks (6 ounces each)1/4 teaspoon salt1/4 teaspoon pepper5 ounces new child spinach (around 6 cups), coarsely cleaved2 cups grape tomatoes, divided1/3 cup arranged pesto1/4 cup slashed pecans1/4 cup disintegrated Gorgonzola cheese

Directions

Cook pasta as indicated by bundle directions.Meanwhile, sprinkle steaks with salt and pepper. Grill steaks, secured, over medium warmth, or cook 4 in. Remove from heat for about 7 minutes on each side or until meat arrives at desired doneness (for medium-uncommon, a thermometer should peruse 135°; medium, 140°; medium-well, 145°).Drain pasta; move to a huge bowl. Include spinach, tomatoes, pesto, and pecans; hurl to cover. Cut steak into thin cuts. Serve pasta blend with hamburger; sprinkle with cheese.

Chicken Alfredo with Grilled Apples

Ingredients

- 4 boneless chicken breast halves4 teaspoons chicken flavoring1 huge Braeburn or Gala apple, cut into 1/2-inch wedges1 tablespoon lemon juice4 cuts provolone cheese1/2 cup Alfredo sauce, warmed1/4 cup disintegrated blue cheese

Directions

Sprinkle the two sides of chicken with chicken flavoring. In a little bowl, hurl apple wedges with lemon juice.Sa paper towel with cooking oil; utilizing since quite a while ago dealt with tongs, rub on grill rack to cover gently. Grill chicken, secured, over medium warmth 5-8 minutes on each side or until a thermometer peruses 165°. Grill apple, achieved, over medium heat 2-3 minutes on each side or until gently sautéed. Top chicken with provolone cheese; cook, secured, 1-2 minutes longer or until cheese is dissolved.Serve chicken with Alfredo sauce and apple. Sprinkle with blue cheese.

Quick Cajun Chicken Penne

Ingredients

- 1 bundle (16 ounces) penne pasta4 boneless chicken breast halves2 teaspoons darkened flavoring2 compartments (10 ounces each) refrigerated Alfredo sauce2 plum tomatoes, hacked3 green onions daintily cut

Directions

Cook pasta as per bundle directions; drain.Soak a paper towel with cooking oil; utilizing since a long time ago took care of tongs, gently coat the grill rack. Sprinkle chicken with darkened flavoring. Grill chicken, over medium heat or broil 4 in. From the warmth for 5-8 minutes on each side or until a thermometer peruses 170°. Cut into reduced down pieces.In a large skillet, heat Alfredo sauce over medium warmth until warm, stirring frequently. Include the tomatoes, onions, pasta, and chicken; toss to coat and heat through.

Creamy Herb-Grilled Herb - Grilled Salmon

Ingredients

- 1/2 cup harsh cream1/4 cup minced crisp chives1/4 cup clipped fresh dill1/4 cup farm serving of mixed greens dressing3 tablespoons minced crisp parsley1 garlic clove, minced1/2 teaspoon prepared salt1/2 teaspoon pepper1 salmon fillet (1 pound)1 teaspoon olive oil

Directions

In a little bowl, blend the first eight ingredients. The brush skin side of salmon with oil.Place salmon on a lubed grill rack, skin side down; spread harsh cream blend over fish. Grill, covered, over medium heat 12-14 minutes or until salmon drops effectively with a fork.

Zesty Grilled Chops

These pork slashes make a brisk organization dish. Our family appreciates them on the grill, as the late spring climate in our part of the nation is hot and moist. In the wintertime, they're fantastically arranged in the grill.

Ingredients

- 3/4 cup soy sauce1/4 cup lemon juice1 tablespoon bean stew sauce1 tablespoon dark colored sugar1 garlic clove, minced6 bone-in pork flank or rib slashes (around 1-1/2 inches thick)

Directions

In a large resealable plastic pack, consolidate the first five ingredients; hold 1/3 cup blend for brushing over slashes. Add pork hacks to sack; seal packet, and go to cover. Refrigerate medium-term.Drain pork, disposing of the marinade. Grill cleaves, secured, over medium heat or cook. from heat until a thermometer peruses 145°, 6-8 minutes for each side. Brush at times withheld soy blend during the most recent 5 minutes. Let stand 5 minutes before serving.

Chicken and Vegetable Kabobs

Ingredients

- 1 pound boneless chicken breast, cut into 1-1/2-inch cubes1 medium sweet red pepper, cut into 1-1/2-inch pieces1 medium zucchini, cut into 1-1/2-inch pieces1 medium red onion, cut into thick wedges2/3 cup sun-dried tomato plate of mixed greens dressing, divided

Directions

In a considerable bowl, join chicken and vegetables. Shower with 1/3 cup wearing and hurl to cover. On the other hand, string chicken and vegetables onto four metal or splashed wooden sticks.Grill kabobs, secured, over medium warmth or sear 4 in. From heat until chicken is never again pink, 8-10 minutes, turning every so often and seasoning with outstanding dressing during the most recent 3 minutes.

Saucy Grilled Baby Back Ribs
Ingredients

- 2 cups ketchup2 cups juice vinegar1 cup of corn syrup1/4 cup pressed dark colored sugar1/4 cup root lager1/2 teaspoon salt1/2 teaspoon garlic powder1/2 teaspoon onion powder1/2 teaspoon hot pepper sauce4 pounds pork infant back ribs

Directions

In a large pan, join the first nine ingredients. Heat to the point of boiling. Diminish excitement; stew, revealed, 20-25 minutes or until somewhat thickened, mixing once in a while.Meanwhile, preheat oven to 325°. Put in a safe spot 3 cups of sauce for treating and serving.Brush remaining sauce over ribs. Spot bone side down on a rack in a large shallow roasting skillet. Spread firmly with foil and heat 1-1/2 to 2 hours or until delicate.On a lubed grill, cook ribs, secured, over medium warmth 15-25 minutes or until caramelized, turning and brushing incidentally with a portion of the saved sauce. Cut into serving-size pieces; present with sauce.

Grilled Steak Bruschetta Salad
Ingredients

- 1-1/2 pounds hamburger tenderloin steaks (1 inch thick)1/2 teaspoon salt1/4 teaspoon pepper6 cups Italian bread (1/2 inch thick)3 cups crisp arugula or baby spinach3/4 cup arranged bruschetta fixing or vegetable salad of your decisionCrumbled blue cheese, discretionary3/4 cup blue cheese serving of mixed greens dressing

Directions

Sprinkle steaks with salt and pepper. Grill, secured, over medium warmth for 6-8 minutes on each side or until meat arrives at desired doneness (for medium-uncommon, a thermometer should peruse 135°; medium, 140°; medium-well, 145°). Let stand for 5 minutes.Grill bread, secured, for 1-2 minutes on each side or until toasted; place on serving of mixed greens plates.Thinly cut steak; orchestrate over toast. Top with arugula and bruschetta beating; sprinkle with cheese whenever wanted. Sprinkle with dressing.

Maple-Thyme Chicken Thighs

Ingredients

- 2 tablespoons stone-ground mustard2 tablespoons maple syrup1 teaspoon minced crisp thyme or 1/2 teaspoon dried thyme1/2 teaspoon salt1/2 teaspoon pepper6 boneless skinless chicken thighs (around 1-1/2 pounds)

Directions

In a little bowl, blend the first five ingredients. Soak a paper towel with cooking oil; utilizing since quite a while ago took care of tongs, rub on grill rack to cover daintily.Grill chicken, secured, over medium warmth 4-5 minutes on each side or until a thermometer peruses 170°. Brush frequently with mustard blend during the most recent 4 minutes of cooking.

Grilled Steak Salad with Tomatoes and Avocado

Ingredients

- 1 meat top sirloin steak (1-1/4 inches thick and 1-1/2 pounds)1 tablespoon olive oil3 teaspoons Creole flavoring2 huge tomatoes, slashed1 can (15 ounces) cannellini beans, washed and depleted1 can (15 ounces) dark beans, rinsed and depleted3 green onions, cleaved1/4 cup minced new cilantro2 teaspoons ground lemon zest2 tablespoons lemon juice1/4 teaspoon salt1 medium ready avocado, stripped and cubed (1/2 inch)

Directions

Rub the two sides of steak with oil; sprinkle with Creole flavoring. Grill, secured, over medium warmth or sear 4 in. From heat 5-8 minutes on each side or until meat arrives at desired doneness (for medium-uncommon, a thermometer should peruse 135°; medium, 140°; medium-well, 145°). Let stand for 5 minutes.In a considerable bowl, join tomatoes, beans, green onions, cilantro, lemon zest, lemon juice, and salt; tenderly mix in avocado. Cut steak into cuts; present with bean blend.

Delicate Pork Chops with Mango Salsa
Ingredients

- 3 tablespoons juice vinegar1 tablespoon sans salt steak-grilling mix1 tablespoon olive oil4 bone-in pork flank hacks (7 ounces each)
- SALSA:
- 2 medium mangoes, stripped and cleaved1 cup cleaved sweet onion1 jalapeno pepper, seeded and finely cleaved1 tablespoon lemon juice2 teaspoons honey

Directions

In an enormous resealable plastic sack, join the vinegar, grilling mix, and oil. Include the pork; seal sack, and go to cover. Refrigerate for at any rate 2 hours.Drain and dispose of the marinade. Grill cleaves, secured, over medium warmth or sear 4-5 in. From the heat for about 5 minutes on each side or until a thermometer peruses 145°. Let represent 5 minutes before serving.Meanwhile, in a little bowl, consolidate the salsa ingredients. Present with chops.

Grilled Shrimp and Peach Kabobs
Ingredients

- 1 tablespoon stuffed sugar1 teaspoon of paprika1 teaspoon of ground ancho bean chili pepper1/2 teaspoon ground cumin1/4 teaspoon salt1/4 teaspoon crisply ground pepper1/4 teaspoon cayenne pepper1 pound of uncooked3 medium peaches, cut into wedges8 green onions, and cut into 2-inch piecesOlive oil-enhanced cooking showerFew Lime wedges

Directions

Mix the sugar and seasonings. Spot peaches, shrimp, and green onions in an enormous bowl; sprinkle it with dark-colored sugar blend and cover. Then again string shrimp, peaches, and green onions.Lightly spritz the two sides of kabobs with cooking shower. Grill, secured, over medium warmth, or cook 4 in. Take from heat for about 4 minutes on each side or until shrimp turn pink. Press lime wedges over kabobs.

Southwest Steak and Potatoes

Striking seasonings give meat and potatoes a Southwest wind. Don't hesitate to change the heat factor by utilizing pretty much bean stew powder.

Ingredients

- 4 medium Yukon Gold potatoes2 teaspoons cider vinegar1 teaspoon Worcestershire sauce1 meat top round steak (1 inch thick and around 1-1/2 pounds)1 tablespoon dark colored sugar1 tablespoon stew powder1-1/2 teaspoons ground cumin1 teaspoon garlic powder1 teaspoon salt, separated1/8 teaspoon cayenne pepper1/8 teaspoon pepper

Directions

Pierce potatoes; place on a microwave-safe plate. Microwave, revealed, on high 4-5 minutes or until practically delicate, turning once. Cool slightly.Meanwhile, blend vinegar and Worcestershire sauce; brush over steak. Blend dark colored sugar, stew powder, cumin, garlic powder, 1/2 teaspoon salt, and cayenne until mixed; sprinkle over the two sides of steak.Cut potatoes into 1/2-in. Sprinkle with pepper and staying salt. Grill potatoes and steak, secured, over medium warmth 12-17 minutes or until vegetables are delicate and a thermometer embedded in meat peruses 145° for medium-uncommon, turning incidentally.Cut steak into thin cuts. Present with potatoes.

Salmon Salad with Glazed Walnuts

Ingredients

- 2 salmon filets (4 ounces each)6 tablespoons decreased fat balsamic vinaigrette, separated1/8 teaspoon pepper4 cups spring blend plate of mixed greens1/4 cup coated pecans2 tablespoons disintegrated blue cheese

Directions

Brush salmon with 2 tablespoons vinaigrette; sprinkle with pepper. On a lubed grill rack, cook salmon, secured, over medium warmth, or sear 4 in. From heat just until fish starts to chip effectively with a fork, 3-4 minutes on each side.In a bowl, prepare to serve of mixed greens with outstanding vinaigrette. The separation between two plates; sprinkle with pecans and cheese. Top with salmon.

Portobello Fajitas
Ingredients

- 3 substantial portobello mushrooms (around 1/2 pound)1 substantial sweet red pepper, cut into strips1/2 huge sweet onion, cut1/2 cup without fat Italian serving of mixed greens dressing2 tablespoons lime juice4 flour tortillas (8 inches), warmed1/2 cup destroyed cheddar cheeseOptional fixings: salsa, guacamole, and harsh cream

Directions

Remove and dispose of stems from mushrooms, with a spoon, scratch, and expel gills. Cut mushrooms into 1/2-in. Cuts and spots in an enormous bowl. Include pepper and onion; shower with salad dressing and hurl to cover. Let stand 10 minutes.Transfer vegetables to a softly lubed grill wok or open grill bin; place on grill rack. Grill, secured, over medium-high warmth 10-12 minutes or until delicate, mixing once in a while.Drizzle vegetables with lime juice. Present with tortillas, cheese, and fixings as wanted.

Ginger Halibut with Brussels Sprouts
Ingredients

- 4 teaspoons lemon juice4 halibut fillets (6 ounces each)1 teaspoon minced new gingerroot1/4 to 3/4 teaspoon salt, partitioned1/4 teaspoon pepper1/2 cup water10 ounces (around 2-1/2 cups) fresh Brussels sprouts, splitCrushed red pepper flakes1 tablespoon canola oil5 garlic cloves, sliced2 tablespoons sesame oil2 tablespoons soy sauceLemon cuts, optional

Directions

Brush lemon squeeze over halibut filets. Sprinkle it with minced ginger, 1/4 teaspoon salt, and pepper.Place fish on an oiled grill rack and skin side down. Grill, secured, over medium warmth (or cook 6 in. from heat) until fish just starts to drop effectively with a fork, 6-8 minutes.In a large skillet, heat water to the point of boiling over medium-high warmth. Include Brussels grows, pepper chips, and, whenever wanted, staying salt. Cook, secured, until delicate, 5-7 minutes. In the interim, in a little skillet, heat oil over medium warmth. Include garlic; cook until brilliant darker. Drain on paper towels.Drizzle sesame oil and soy sauce over halibut. Present with Brussels grows; sprinkle with seared garlic. Whenever wanted, gift with lemon cuts.

Grilled Huli Huli Chicken

Ingredients

- 1 cup stuffed dark colored sugar3/4 cup ketchup3/4 cup decreased sodium soy sauce1/3 cup sherry or chicken soup2-1/2 teaspoons minced new gingerroot1-1/2 teaspoons minced garlic24 boneless skinless chicken thighs (around 5 pounds)

Directions

In a little bowl, blend the first six ingredients. Save 1-1/3 cups for seasoning; cover and refrigerate. Gap remaining marinade between two enormous resealable plastic sacks. Add 12 chicken thighs to each; seal packs and go to cover. Refrigerate for 8 hours or medium-term.Drain and dispose of the marinade from chicken.Grill chicken, secured, on an oiled rack over medium warmth for 6-8 minutes on each side or until never again pink; season once in a while withheld marinade during the most recent 5 minutes.

Honey Glazed Chicken Kabobs

Ingredients

- 2/3 cup diminished sodium soy sauce2/3 cup nectar1/2 cup canola oil1 tablespoon arranged horseradish2 teaspoons steak flavoring2 garlic cloves, minced2 pounds boneless chicken bosoms, cut into 1-1/2-inch shapes1 enormous sweet red pepper, cut into 1-1/2-inch pieces1 immense green pepper, cut into 1-1/2-inch pieces1 colossal onion, cut into 1-1/2-inch wedges

Directions

In a little bowl, join the first six ingredients. Empty 1 cup marinade into a substantial resealable plastic sack; include the chicken. Seal bag and go to cover; refrigerate for 5-6 hours. Cover and refrigerate remaining marinade.Drain and dispose of the marinade. On six metal or splashed wooden sticks, on the other hand, string chicken and vegetables. Grill, secured, over medium warmth for 5-7 minutes on each side or until chicken juices run clear, seasoning now and again with saved marinade.

Grilled Tilapia Piccata
Ingredients

- 1/2 teaspoon ground lemon pizzazz3 tablespoons lemon juice2 tablespoons olive oil2 garlic cloves, minced2 teaspoons escapades, depleted3 tablespoons minced crisp basil, separated4 tilapia fillets (6 ounces each)1/2 teaspoon salt1/4 teaspoon pepper

Directions

In a little bowl, whisk lemon pizzazz, lemon juice, oil, and garlic until mixed, mix in tricks and 2 tablespoons basil. Hold two tablespoons blend for showering cooked fish. Brush remaining mixture onto the two sides of tilapia; sprinkle with salt and pepper.Grill tilapia on a softly oiled rack, secured, over medium warmth, or cook 4 in. From heat until fish just starts to chip effectively with a fork, 3-4 minutes on each side. Shower with a saved lemon blend; sprinkle with outstanding basil.

Honey-Chipotle Ribs
Ingredients

- 6 pounds pork baby back ribs
- BARBECUE SAUCE:
- 3 cups ketchup2 bottles (11.2 ounces every) Guinness brew2 cups grill sauce2/3 cup nectar1 little onion, hacked1/4 cup Worcestershire sauce2 tablespoons Dijon mustard2 tablespoons of diced chipotle peppers in adobo sauce4 teaspoons ground chipotle pepper1 teaspoon salt
- 1 teaspoon garlic powder1/2 teaspoon pepper

Directions

Wrap ribs in huge bits of rock-solid foil; seal edges of foil. Grill, secured, over backhanded medium warmth for 1 to 1-1/2 hours or until delicate.In a huge pan, join sauce ingredients; heat to the point of boiling. Decrease heat; stew, revealed, for around 45 minutes or until thickened, mixing sporadically.Carefully expel ribs from foil. Spot over direct warmth; season with a portion of the sauce. Grill, secured, over medium heat for around 30 minutes or until cooked, turning once and treating at times with extra sauce. Present with remaining sauce.

Grilled Veggie Pizza
Ingredients
- 8 little crisp mushrooms, divided1 small zucchini, cut into 1/4-inch cuts1 little sweet yellow pepper, cut1 little fresh red pepper, cut1 little onion, cut1 tablespoon white wine vinegar1 tablespoon water4 teaspoons olive oil, partitioned2 teaspoons minced crisp basil or 1/2 teaspoon dried basil1/4 teaspoon salt1/4 teaspoon pepper1 prebaked 12-inch slight entire wheat pizza covering1 can (8 ounces) pizza sauce2 little tomatoes, cleaved2 cups destroyed part-skim mozzarella cheese

Directions
In an enormous bowl, join the mushrooms, zucchini, peppers, onion, vinegar, water, 3 teaspoons oil, and seasonings. Move to a grill wok or bushel. Grill, secured, over medium warmth for 8-10 minutes or until delicate, mixing once.Get ready grill for backhanded warmth. Brush covering with residual oil; spread with pizza sauce. Top with grilled vegetables, tomatoes, and cheese. Grill, secured, over roundabout medium warmth for 10-12 minutes or until edges are daintily caramelized, and cheese is dissolved. Turn pizza part of the way through cooking to guarantee uniformly sautéed outside layer.

Brown Sugar Salmon with Strawberries
Ingredients
- 1/3 cup stuffed dark colored sugar1 tablespoon canola oil1 teaspoon ground mustard1 teaspoon ground allspice1/2 teaspoon salt4 salmon filets (5 ounces each)

RELISH:
- 1 tablespoon minced new mint1 tablespoon canola oil1 tablespoon lemon juice2 teaspoons ground lemon get-up-and-go1/8 teaspoon sugar1 cup finely hacked crisp strawberries1 little cucumber, finely hacked

Directions
In a small bowl, blend the first five ingredients; rub over tissue side of salmon. Refrigerate, secured, 60 minutes.For relish, in another bowl, combine mint, oil, lemon juice, lemon strip and sugar. Include strawberries and cucumber; hurl to cover.Lightly oil grill rack. Spot salmon on grill rack, skin side down. Grill, secured, over medium warmth 8-10 minutes or until fish drops effectively with a fork. Present with relish.

Lemon Chicken Skewers

Ingredients

- 1/4 cup olive oil3 tablespoons lemon juice1 tablespoon white wine vinegar2 garlic cloves, minced

- 2 teaspoons ground lemon pizzazz1 teaspoon salt1/2 teaspoon sugar1/4 teaspoon dried oregano1/4 teaspoon pepper1-1/2 pounds boneless skinless chicken bosoms, cut into 1-1/2-in. pieces3 medium zucchini, divided the long way and cut into 1-1/2-inch cuts3 medium onions, cut into wedges12 cherry tomatoes

Directions

In an enormous bowl, consolidate the first nine ingredients; put aside 1/4 cup for seasoning. Empty half into a massive pot. Include chicken; go to cover. Empty the rest of the marinade into another considerable bowl. Include the zucchini, onions, and tomatoes; go to cover. Cover and refrigerate chicken and vegetables for as long as 4 hours or medium-term.Drain and dispose of the marinade. On the other hand, string chicken and vegetables onto metal or splashed wooden sticks. Grill, secured, over medium warmth for 6 minutes on each side or until chicken juices run clear, seasoning periodically with saved marinade.

Maple and Blue Cheese Steak
This is a superb, gooey recipe that melts in your mouth. I love this conventional Canadian meal. It unquestionably has an exceptional vibe; the sauce is a phenomenal supplement to steak.

Ingredients

- 6 tablespoons balsamic vinegar6 tablespoons maple syrup, separated2 tablespoons in addition to 1-1/2 teaspoons Dijon mustard1 tablespoon minced new thyme or 1/4 teaspoon dried thyme1/2 pound meat top sirloin steak2 tablespoons hacked walnuts1-1/2 teaspoons olive oil1/8 teaspoon salt1/8 teaspoon pepper1/4 cup disintegrated blue cheese

Directions

In a little bowl, consolidate the vinegar, 5 tablespoons maple syrup, mustard, and thyme. Pour 2/3 cup of marinade into a shallow dish; add the steak and go to cover. Cover and refrigerate for as long as 3 hours. Cover and refrigerate remaining marinade.Meanwhile, in a little skillet, sauté walnuts in oil until toasted. Mix in outstanding maple syrup. Heat to the point of boiling; cook for 1 moment, mixing always. Expel from skillet and spread onto waxed paper to cool totally.Drain and dispose of the marinade. Sprinkle steak with salt and pepper. Grill, over medium warmth, for 4-6 minutes on each side or until meat arrives at desired doneness (for medium-uncommon, a thermometer should peruse 135°; medium, 140°; medium-well, 145°). Let represent 5 minutes before cutting.The place held marinade in a little pan. Heat to the point of boiling; cook until fluid is diminished to 1/4 cup, around 2 minutes. Separation steak cuts between two plates. Shower with sauce; sprinkle with blue cheese and walnuts.

Lime-Glazed Pork Chops

These tart grilled slashes are all the discussion at grills and rear ends. You have to have them with sweet and sour glaze.

Ingredients

- 1/3 cup orange preserves1 jalapeno pepper, seeded and finely slashed2 tablespoons lime juice1 teaspoon ground crisp gingerroot4 bone-in pork flank hacks (8 ounces each)4 teaspoons minced crisp cilantroLime wedges

Directions

For the coat, in a little pan, consolidate jelly, jalapeno, lime squeeze, and ginger; cook and mix over medium warmth 4-6 minutes or until preserves are softened.Soak a paper towel with cooking oil; utilizing since quite a while ago took care of tongs, rub on grill rack to cover delicately.Grill slashes, secured, over medium warmth or sear 4 in. From heat 6-8 minutes on each side or until a thermometer peruses 145°, brushing with a coat during the most recent 5 minutes. Let stand for 5 minutes. Sprinkle with cilantro; present with lime wedges.

Steak Kabobs

These steak kabobs not just fulfill my adoration for open-air cooking, and they highlight a delicious marinade, as well. It's marvelous with chicken and pork, yet I lean toward it with meat since it kneads amazingly well.

Ingredients

- 1/2 cup canola oil1/4 cup soy sauce3 tablespoons nectar2 tablespoons white vinegar1/2 teaspoon ground ginger1/2 teaspoon garlic powder1-1/2 pounds meat top sirloin steak, cut into 1-inch shapes1/2 pound entire new mushrooms2 medium onions, cut into wedges1 sweet red pepper, then cut into 1-inch pieces1 medium green pepper, cut into 1-inch pieces1 medium yellow squash, cut into 1/2-inch cutsHot cooked rice

Directions

In an enormous bowl, consolidate the first six ingredients. Include meat; go to cover. Cover and refrigerate 8 hours or medium-term.On 12 metal or drenched wooden sticks, on the other hand, string hamburger and vegetables, dispose of the marinade. Grill kabobs, secured, over medium warmth until meat arrives at desired doneness, 10-12 minutes, turning at times. Present with rice.

Blackened Chicken

This fiery darkened chicken sneaks up all of a sudden of flavor. The grilled chicken is seasoned with a peppery white sauce—there's a lot of additional sauce leftover for plunging.

Ingredients

- 1 tablespoon paprika4 teaspoons sugar, separated1-1/2 teaspoons salt, separated1 teaspoon garlic powder1 teaspoon dried thyme1 teaspoon lemon-pepper flavoring1 teaspoon cayenne pepper1-1/2 to 2 teaspoons pepper, separated4 boneless skinless chicken breast halves (4 ounces each)1-1/3 cups mayonnaise2 tablespoons water2 tablespoons juice vinegar

Directions

In a little bowl, consolidate the paprika, 1 teaspoon sugar, 1 teaspoon salt, garlic powder, thyme, lemon-pepper, cayenne, and 1/2 to 1 teaspoon pepper; sprinkle over the two sides of chicken. Put in a safe spot.In another bowl, consolidate the mayonnaise, water, vinegar, and remaining sugar, salt, and pepper; cover and refrigerate 1 cup for serving. Extra outstanding sauce for seasoning.Grill chicken, secured, over circuitous medium warmth for 4-6 minutes on each side or until a thermometer peruses 170°, seasoning much of the time with outstanding sauce. Present with held sauce.

Barbeque Alaskan Salmon
Ingredients

- 2 tablespoons margarine2 tablespoons darker sugar1 to 2 garlic cloves1 tablespoon of lemon juice2 teaspoons of soy sauce1/2 teaspoon of pepper4 salmon steaks

Directions

In a little pan, consolidate the first six ingredients. Cook and mix until sugar is broken down.Meanwhile, grill salmon, secured, over medium-hot warmth for 5 minutes. Turn salmon; season with the spread sauce. Grill 7-9 minutes longer, turning and seasoning at times, or until the salmon drops effectively with a fork.

Butterly Grilled Shrimp

This is simple and flavorful! These shrimp are incredible with steak. However, for an extraordinary event, brush the sauce on lobster tails and grill.

Ingredients

- 1/2 cup margarine, dissolved3 tablespoons lemon juice2 teaspoons stew powder1 teaspoon ground ginger1/4 teaspoon salt2 pounds uncooked shrimp (16-20 for each pound), stripped and deveined

Directions

In a little bowl, consolidate the first 5 ingredients; put aside 1/4 cup. String shrimp onto 8 metal or doused wooden sticks.Grill shrimp, secured, over medium warmth 3-5 minutes on each side or until shrimp turn pink, treating periodically with margarine blend. Expel from grill; brush with held butter mixture.

Blue Cheese Flat Iron Steak

This is one of my preferred level iron steak recipes. If you haven't just appreciated the rich, velvety pairing of blue cheese with your preferred steak, quit perusing, and get cooking! Make it a stride further by collapsing in a little margarine to make the dish considerably more slobber commendable.

Ingredients

- 1/4 cup olive oil2 tablespoons red wine vinegar2 garlic cloves, minced1 teaspoon dried oregano1 teaspoon dried rosemary, squashed1 teaspoon pepper1/4 teaspoon salt1-1/4 pounds hamburger level iron steak or top sirloin steak (1 inch thick)

Blue Cheese Butter:

- 1/4 cup disintegrated blue cheese3 tablespoons margarine, mollified1 tablespoon minced crisp chives1/8 teaspoon pepper

Directions

In a shallow dish, join the first seven ingredients. Include meat; go to cover. Cover and refrigerate 30 minutes.In a little bowl, blend blue cheese, margarine, chives, and pepper; put in a safe spot. Channel meat, disposing of the marinade.Grill steaks, secured, over medium warmth or sear 4 in. From heat for about 8 minutes on each side or until beef arrives at desired doneness (for medium-uncommon, a thermometer should peruse 135°; medium, 140°; medium-well, 145°). Present with blue cheese margarine.

Ricotta-Stuffed Portobello Mushrooms

These mushrooms are luxurious and velvety and splendid simultaneously in light of the fresh herbs and tomato. I mainly prefer to serve them with grilled asparagus.

Ingredients

- 3/4 cup diminished fat ricotta cheese3/4 cup ground Parmesan cheese, partitioned1/2 cup destroyed part-skim mozzarella cheese2 tablespoons minced crisp parsley1/8 teaspoon pepper6 enormous portobello mushrooms6 cuts a massive tomato3/4 cup fresh basil leaves3 tablespoons fragmented almonds or pine nuts, toasted1 small garlic clove2 tablespoons olive oil2 to 3 teaspoons water

Directions

In a little bowl, blend ricotta cheese, 1/4 cup Parmesan cheese, mozzarella cheese, parsley, and pepper. Expel and dispose of stems from mushrooms; with a spoon, scratch, and evacuate gills. Fill tops with ricotta blend. Top with tomato cuts.Grill, secured, over medium warmth until mushrooms are delicate, 8-10 minutes. Expel from the grill with a metal spatula.Meanwhile, place basil, almonds, and garlic in a little food processor; beat until cleaved. Include remaining Parmesan cheese; beat just until mixed. While preparing, bit by bit add oil and enough water to arrive at the desired consistency. Spoon overstuffed mushrooms before serving.

Grilled Greek Pita Pizzas

This simple flatbread pizza catches great Mediterranean flavors in each nibble. It works similarly well as a rapid primary dish or a starter.

Ingredients

- 1 container (12 ounces) marinated quartered artichoke hearts, depleted and cleaved1 cup grape tomatoes, split1/2 cup pitted Greek olives, split1/3 cup cleaved crisp parsley2 tablespoons olive oil1/4 teaspoon pepper3/4 cup hummus4 entire pita bread1 cup disintegrated feta cheese

Directions

Place the first six ingredients in a little bowl; hurl to consolidate. Spread hummus over pita bread. Top with artichoke blend; sprinkle with cheese. Grill pizzas, secured, over medium warmth until bottoms are brilliant darker, 4-5 minutes.

Grilled Tilapia with Pineapple Salsa
Ingredients

- 2 cups cubed crisp pineapple2 green onions, cleaved1/4 cup finely cleaved green pepper1/4 cup minced crisp cilantro4 teaspoons in addition to 2 tablespoons lime juice, partitioned1/8 teaspoon in addition to 1/4 teaspoon salt, partitionedDash cayenne pepper1 tablespoon canola oil8 tilapia fillets (4 ounces each)1/8 teaspoon pepper

Directions

For salsa, in a little bowl, join pineapple, green onions, green pepper, cilantro, 4 teaspoons lime juice, 1/8 teaspoon salt, and cayenne. Refrigerate until serving.Mix oil and remaining lime juice; shower over filets. Sprinkle with pepper and staying salt.Moisten a paper towel with cooking oil, since quite a while ago took care of tongs, rub on grill rack to cover softly. Grill fish, secured, over medium warmth or sear 4 in. Remove from heat 2-3 minutes on each side or until fish just starts to chip effectively with a fork. Present with salsa.

Spicy Barbecued Chicken
This hot, saucy chicken is incredibly presented with basil-buttered grilled natural corn and new coleslaw.

Ingredients

- 1 tablespoon canola oil2 garlic cloves, minced1/2 cup stew sauce3 tablespoons dark colored sugar2 teaspoons sans salt flavoring mix, partitioned3/4 teaspoon cayenne pepper, isolated2 teaspoons ground mustard2 teaspoons bean stew powder8 boneless skinless chicken breast halves (4 ounces each)

Directions

In a little pan, heat oil over medium warmth. Include garlic; cook and mix 1 moment. Include bean stew sauce, dark colored sugar, 1 teaspoon flavoring mix, and 1/4 teaspoon cayenne. Heat to the point of boiling; cook and combination for 1 moment. Expel from heat.In a little bowl, blend mustard, stew powder, and remaining flavoring mix and cayenne; rub over chicken. Delicately cover grill rack with cooking oil.Grill chicken, secured, over medium warmth for 4 minutes. Turn; grill 4-6 minutes longer or until a thermometer peruses 165°, brushing tops sporadically with bean stew sauce blend.

CHAPTER FOUR GRILLED APPETIZER RECIPES

Grilled Appetizer Party Pointers

1. Offer the work. There's consistently that companion who asks how he/she can help. Take them up on it and transform party-prep into a pre-funk as you hack, stick, and marinate. Have beverages, snacks, and music close by to fuel the good times.**2. The amount to make**. Plan to serve in any event 5 various types of appetizers for a gathering of 10 to 12 individuals. For more individuals, increment the number of appetizers.**3. Blend it up**. Incorporate appetizers that don't need to be grilled, so visitors have things to snack on while the cooked foods are on the grill. Attempt cheeses, plunges, nuts, and so on.

Grilled Tequila-Lime Shrimp

<u>Lime and tequila-marinated shrimp grilled on sticks make a simple appetizer to appreciate all mid-year.</u>

Ingredients

- 2 tablespoons lime juice2 tablespoons tequila1/4 cup olive oil1 squeeze garlic salt1 squeeze ground cuminground dark pepper to taste1 pound enormous shrimp, stripped and deveined6 (10 inches) wooden sticks1 massive lime, quartered

Instructions

Mix together the olive oil, garlic salt, lime juice, tequila, cumin, and dark pepper in a bowl until very much mixed. Fill a large resealable plastic pack, including the shrimp, seal sack, and go to cover equally. Refrigerate 1 to 4 hours before grilling.Soak sticks in any event 30 minutes in water to forestall consuming.Preheat outside grill for medium-high warmth. Daintily oil grill mesh, and spot around 4 creeps from heat source.Drain and dispose of the marinade from shrimp. String shrimp onto arranged sticks, 5 to 6 for every stick.Cook, revealed, on the preheated grill until shrimp turn pink, turning once, for 5 to 7 minutes. Present with lime wedges for garnish.

Thai Chicken Satay

Prep is brisk best whenever left to marinade for a couple of hours or more. Stick up for the grill or sauté on the stove! I purchase the chicken tenderloin strips, which areas of now boned, cleaned, and a decent size piece without cutting to spare time.

Ingredients

- ½ cup of canned coconut milk1 ½ teaspoon ground coriander1 teaspoon yellow curry powder1 teaspoon fish sauce½ teaspoon bean stew oil1 pound skinless, boneless chicken bosom parts - cut into strips1 tablespoon slashed crisp cilantro1 tablespoon slashed unsalted peanuts12 wooden sticks, absorbed water for 15 minutes1 cup arranged Thai peanut sauce

Directions

In a medium bowl, mix the coconut milk, ground coriander, curry powder, fish sauce, and bean stew oil. Include the chicken bosom strips, and mix to cover. Spread, and refrigerate for at any rate 30 minutes, and as long as 2 hours.Preheat an indoor or open-air grill for high warmth. String the chicken strips onto sticks. Dispose of the marinade.Grill chicken for 2 to 3 minutes for every side, until never again pink. Time will rely upon how thick your strips are. Move to a serving plate and enhancement with cilantro and peanuts. Present with peanut sauce for dipping.

Pesto-Stuffed Grilled Portobellos

Pesto-stuffed grilled portobellos make for the ideal summer open-air meal. It remains solitary as a vegetarian passage if you serve it with a crisp natural product, (for example, watermelon lumps and blueberries); I love it with cedar-plank grilled salmon too. You will think you've kicked the bucket and gone to paradise.

Ingredients

- 6 portobello mushrooms1 tablespoon olive oil1 little shallot, minced1 clove garlic, minced1 sprinkle Chardonnay wine, or as wanted3 tablespoons pesto2 tablespoons pine nuts

Instructions

Remove stems from the mushrooms and neatly chop the stems.Heat the olive oil in a skillet over medium warmth; cook and mix cleaved mushroom stems, shallot, and garlic until mellowed, around 5 minutes. Empty wine into the skillet; cook and mix blend utilizing a wooden spoon until fluid is dissipated, 1 to 2 minutes. Refreshing blend to room temperature, around 10 minutes.Preheat an open-air grill for medium warmth and gently oil the mesh.Brush the olive oil blend super each mushroom and spot, top-side up, on a grilling container. Blend pesto and pine nuts with the mushroom stem blend together in a bowl; spoon into each mushroom. Sprinkle Italian cheese mix over the filling.Grill the mushrooms on the preheated grill until edges are darkened, and stuffing is rising around 10 minutes.

Grilled Eggplant Rollups

<u>Delicious grilled eggplant supplements the kinds of goat cheese and cooked red pepper in this 'couldn't be simpler' recipe that is acceptable served hot, cold, or as scraps. To re-warm, place on a low-heat grill for 2 minutes.</u>

Ingredients

- 1 eggplant, stripped and cut the long way into 1/4-inch cutssalt varying1 tablespoon olive oil, or varying1 squeeze Italian flavoring, or to taste1 (4 ounces) log goat cheese, mellowed2 canned entire cooked red peppers, depleted and diced

Instructions

Arrange eggplant cuts on a huge plate and sprinkle with salt. Cook until water has been drawn out, at any rate, 30 minutes. Wash eggplant cuts and pat dry with a paper towel.Preheat grill for medium warmth and softly oil the mesh.Lightly brush the two sides of eggplant cuts with olive oil and season with Italian flavoring.Grill eggplant cuts on the preheated grill, precisely 3 minutes for every side. Spread goat cheese on 1 side of every eggplant cut and sprinkle with broiled red peppers. Serve open-confronted or moved up.

Grilled Prosciutto and Peach Flatbread Pizza

Delicate naan beat with a light spread of ricotta, bested with sweet peaches, salty prosciutto, a little basil, and a sprinkle of nectar balsamic decrease - all grilled to flawlessness!

Ingredients

- 1 cup balsamic vinegar1/4 cup honey1/2 teaspoon lemon juice1/4 teaspoon dark pepper2 naan bread4 ounces ricotta cheese2 new peaches, cut1 (3 ounces) bundle prosciutto, attacked pieces3 tablespoons daintily cut fresh basil

Instructions

Combine balsamic vinegar, nectar, lemon squeeze, and pepper in a little pot. Heat to point of boiling over high warmth; diminish to low. Stew until blend has decreased down to 1/3 cup, around 15 minutes.Preheat an open-air grill for medium-high heat and delicately oil the mesh.Grill naan until blackout scorch marks show up, 2 to 3 minutes. Spread ricotta cheese over the scorched side. Top with peaches and prosciutto. Sprinkle with basil. Shower with balsamic decrease.Return flatbreads to the grill. Grill with the spread on, until the cheese is liquefied and the base of the flatbread starts to scorch, around 7 minutes.

Grilled Tofu Skewers with Sriracha Sauce
Ingredients
Unique recipe yields 2 servings

- 1 (8 ounces) holder additional firm tofu, depleted and cut into huge pieces1 zucchini, cut into enormous pieces1 red ringer pepper, cut into huge pieces10 enormous mushrooms2 tablespoons sriracha bean stew garlic sauce¼ cup of soy sauce2 tablespoons sesame oil¼ cup diced onion1 jalapeno pepper, dicedground dark pepper to taste

Directions

Spot tofu, zucchini, red ringer pepper, and mushrooms in a bowl. Blend sriracha sauce, soy sauce, sesame oil, onion, jalapeno, and pepper in a little bowl, and pour over tofu and vegetables. Hurl daintily to cover. Spread, and permit to marinate in any event 1 hour in the cooler.Preheat an outside grill for medium-high warmth, and daintily oil the mesh.String tofu and vegetables on to skewer. Grill each for 10 minutes or to desired doneness. Utilize any outstanding marinade as a plunging sauce.

Grill Master Chicken Wings

These wings are always a hit! I grill them up before a gathering and keep them hot in a low oven. It has loads of flavor and isn't excessively zesty.

IngredientsWings:

- ½ cup of soy sauce½ cup Italian-style serving of mixed greens dressing3 pounds chicken wings, cut separated at joints, wing tips disposed of

Sauce:

- ¼ cup spread1 teaspoon soy sauce¼ cup hot pepper sauce

Directions

Consolidate 1/2 cup soy sauce, Italian dressing, and chicken wings in an enormous, zip-top sack. Close sack and refrigerate 4 hours to medium-term.Preheat an open-air grill for medium warmth. In a little pan, dissolve the spread. Mix in the 1 teaspoon soy sauce and the hot pepper sauce: mood killer heat and hold.Expel the chicken wings from the marinade and pat dry. Cook the sides on the preheated grill, turning once in a while, until the chicken is very much caramelized and never again pink, 25 to 30 minutes.Spot grilled wings in an enormous bowl. Pour spread sauce over wings; hurl to blend well.

Marinated Chicken Kabobs

This extraordinary summer recipe was given to me by companion years back. You can put any vegetables you need on the sticks. Try not to be concerned when you see the light corn syrup in the ingredients, and it meets up extraordinary! It's a remarkable change. You can even skirt the vegetables and simply stick the chicken. Appreciate!

Ingredients

- 1 cup of vegetable oil½ cup of soy sauce½ cup light corn syrup¼ cup lemon juice2 tablespoons sesame seeds½ teaspoon garlic powdergarlic salt to taste4 skinless, boneless chicken bosom parts - cut into 1/2 inch pieces1 (8 ounces) bundle new hacked mushrooms2 onions, quartered1 green chime pepper, cut into huge lumps

Directions

In a medium bowl, mix vegetable oil, soy sauce, light corn syrup, lemon juice, sesame seeds, garlic powder, and garlic salt. Spot chicken in the blend. Spread, and marinate in the cooler at any rate 2 hours.Preheat an open-air grill for medium warmth, and daintily oil grind. String chicken onto sticks, on the other hand, with mushrooms, onions, and green ringer pepper. Dry marinade into a pan and heat to the point of boiling. Cook for 5 to 10 minutes.Spot sticks on the readied grill. Cook 15 to 20 minutes, turning much of the time until chicken is never again pink and squeezes run clear. Treat with the bubbled marinade as often as possible during the most recent 10 minutes.

Steak on a Stick

A speedy and straightforward, exceptionally delicious variant of the teriyaki steak-on-a-stick that you get from a Chinese eatery. It's incredible as a tidbit or even as finger food at a football-watching party! I likewise use it for out and out old customary steaks to grill! In any case, it's lovely!

Ingredients

- 1/2 cup soy sauce1/4 cup olive oil1/4 cup water2 tablespoons molasses2 teaspoons mustard powder1 teaspoon ground ginger1/2 teaspoon garlic powder1/2 teaspoon onion powder2 pounds flank steak, cut into slight strips32 wooden sticks (8 inches since quite a while ago) absorbed water

Instructions

In a large resealable pack, consolidate the soy sauce, olive oil, water, molasses, mustard powder, ginger, garlic powder, and onion powder. Seal and shake the pack to combine. Add steak strips to the package and seal. Refrigerate for at any rate 8 hours to marinate.Preheat the oven's grill. String meat onto sticks and place on a broiling rack.Broil the steak for 3 to 4 minutes on each side. Organize on a platter to serve.

Strawberry Goat Cheese Bruschetta

The way the tart, somewhat salty goat cheese works with the syrupy, balsamic-covered strawberries and firm, singed bread is a beautiful thing.

Ingredients

- 1/2 cup balsamic vinegar12 cups Italian bread1 tablespoon olive oil1 pound strawberries, washed and diced2 teaspoons new thyme leaves, in addition to additional for serving1 cup goat cheese, room temperaturesalt and newly ground pepper to taste

Instructions

Heat vinegar in a little skillet over medium-low warmth. Stew until decreased by about half, 8 to 10 minutes. Expel from warmth and permit to cool to room temperature.Prepare a grill for high heat. Spot bread cuts on a foil-fixed baking sheet and shower with olive oil.Combine strawberries and thyme in a little bowl and put them in a safe spot.Grill bread on the preheated grill until sautéed, around 3 minutes for every side.Spread goat cheese on toasted bread. Include dark pepper, salt, and decreased vinegar to the strawberry blend. Spoon over the goat cheese beet bruschetta. Embellishment with extra thyme.

Shrimp and Scallops with Lemony Soy

The Japanese-style marinade here works particularly fast, because of the blend of tart citrus and salty soy sauce.

Ingredients

- 1 1/2 cups low-sodium soy sauce1 cup mirin1 cup purpose2 lemons, daintily cut2 jalapeños, daintily cut1 pound medium shrimp, shelled and deveined1 pound huge ocean scallopsVegetable oil, for grilling

The most effective method to make It

In a glass or earthenware baking dish, join the soy sauce with the mirin, purpose, lemon cuts, and jalapeños.String the shrimp onto 8 pairs of bamboo sticks and add them to the marinade, going to cover. Rehash with the scallops. Cool the seafood for 30 minutes, turning once part of the way through, at that point channel.Light a grill and oil the meshes. Brush shrimp and scallops with oil, and then grill over high warmth, turning a few times, until delicately roasted, around 4 minutes. Serve immediately.

Grilled-Vegetable Gazpacho

Exemplary Andalusian gazpacho joins raw vegetables like tomatoes and onions with red wine vinegar for a little kick. Changes the recipe by utilizing grilled vegetables lit up with a mix of vinegar, squeezed orange and lemon juice.

Ingredients

- 4 enormous garlic cloves, unpeeled2 enormous red ringer peppers, cored and quartered2 enormous yellow ringer peppers, cored and quartered2 medium zucchini, cut the long way 1/2 inch thick1 massive white onion, cut into 1/2-inch sections2 ears of corn, husked2 tablespoons vegetable oilKosher salt and naturally ground pepper1 1/2 teaspoons ground cumin1/2 teaspoon squashed red pepper2 cups tomato juice1/2 cup crisp squeezed orange3 tablespoons crisp lemon juice2 tablespoons red wine vinegar1/4 cup packed cilantro1 English cucumber, daintily cut

The most effective method to make it

Light a grill. String the garlic cloves onto a stick. Daintily brush the garlic, chime peppers, zucchini, onion, and corn with the vegetable oil and season with salt and pepper. Grill the vegetables over tolerably high warmth, often turning, until gently singed and fresh delicate, around 10 minutes. Move the peppers to a bowl, spread with plastic, and let steam for 10 minutes.In the interim, expel the garlic cloves from the sticks, strip them and move to a huge bowl. Utilizing an enormous serrated blade, cut the scorched corn bits into the container. Strip the peppers and add them to the bowl alongside the zucchini, onion, cumin, squashed red pepper, tomato juice, squeezed orange, lemon juice, and vinegar.Working in groups, puree the vegetable blend in a blender or food processor. Empty the gazpacho into a perfect bowl and season with salt and pepper. Cover and refrigerate until chilled, around 2 hours.Just before serving, mix the cilantro into the gazpacho. Spoon the soup into bowls, embellish with the cucumber and serve.

Sausage Lovers' Grilled Pizza

This is a definitive summer pizza, bested with heaps of ground summer squash and interesting pepperoncini, alongside frankfurter.

Ingredients

- 1 pound summer squash (around 2), ground on the enormous gaps of a crate grater1/2 teaspoon fit salt, in addition to additional for flavoring2 tablespoons extra-virgin olive oil, in addition to extra for brushingOne 14-ounce can diced tomatoes, depletedPinch of sugarOne 1-pound chunk of pizza mixture, defrosted whenever solidifiedOne 8-ounce ball crisp mozzarella, meagerly cut2 cooked frankfurters from Mixed Grill, meagerly cut4 pepperoncini, stemmed and meagerly cutBasil leaves, for decorate

The most effective method to make it

Light a grill. Hurl the squash with the 1/2 teaspoon of salt; let represent 15 minutes, at that point crush out the abundance fluid.In a substantial nonstick skillet, heat the 2 tablespoons of olive oil until shining. Include the squash and cook over reasonably high warmth just until brilliant in spots, 3 minutes.In a food processor, beat the tomatoes until practically smooth; season the tomato sauce with salt and the sugar.On a delicately floured work surface, reveal the pizza batter to a 1/4-inch-thick round or oval. Brush the butter with olive oil and oil the hot grill grind. Wrap the mixture, oiled side down, onto the hot mesh. Grill over moderate warmth until marks show up on the base, and the dough is somewhat firm and puffed around 3 minutes. Turn the mixture over onto a treat sheet and brush with olive oil. Spread the tomato sauce over the mixture, leaving a 1-inch fringe. Disperse the squash over the pizza and top with the cut mozzarella cheese and frankfurters.Slide the pizza back onto the grill. Spread the grill and cook until the outside layer is done and the cheese is softened around 5 minutes. Move the pizza to a platter, decorate with the pepperoncini and basil and serve.

Smoking' Sweet Chicken Wings with Cherry Barbecue Glaze

Cherry jam with habanero chile makes a spectacularly clingy, sweet, and fiery coating for grilled chicken wings. Coating them just before serving, so the sugars don't consume.

Ingredients

- 2 tablespoons unsalted margarine1/2 medium sweet onion, for example, Vidalia, finely slashed1 enormous habanero chile, seeded and minced3/4 cup cherry jam, ideally harsh cherry1/3 cup crisp lime juiceSaltFreshly ground dark pepper3 1/2 pounds chicken wings, tips disposed of and sides split

The most effective method to make it

In a medium pot, liquefy the margarine. Include the slashed sweet onion and cook over moderate warmth, blending once in a while, until the onion is mellowed and softly seared, around 5 minutes. Include three-fourths of the minced habanero chile and cook for 1 moment, just until relaxed. Scratch the onion and habanero into a blender, include the cherry jam and lime squeeze and puree until smooth. Return the cherry coating to the pot and heat it to the point of boiling over reasonably high warmth. Mix in the remaining minced habanero chile and season the surface with salt and dark pepper. Move the coating to a little bowl.Light a grill or preheat an oven and position a rack 8 crawls from the warmth source. Season the chicken wings done with salt and dark pepper and grill over decently high warmth, turning once in a while, until softly singed and fresh, around 20 minutes. On the other hand, cook the wings for approximately 20 minutes, turning once in a while, until they are clean.Move the chicken wings to an enormous bowl and hurl with 33% of the cherry coating. Cook after returning the wings to the grill, turning once, just until clingy and caramelized, around 2 minutes. Return the chicken wings to the bowl and hurl with another third of the cherry coating. Move the coated chicken wings to a serving platter and present with the rest of the surface as an afterthought.

Grilled Beef Rolls
Simple Way Grape leaves make a phenomenal swap for la parcel in these crunchy grilled meat rolls.

Ingredients

- 1/4 cup in addition to 1 tablespoon vegetable oil, in addition to additional for brushing1 tablespoon Asian fish sauce1 crisp lemongrass stalk, delicate internal white bulb just, minced1/2 teaspoon five-zest powder1 1/2 teaspoons nectar4 garlic cloves—1 minced, 3 meagerly cutKosher salt1/2 pound flank steak, meagerly cut over the grain into 1/4-inch-thick cuts, at that point split across12 enormous grape leaves from a container1/2 little jicama, stripped and cut into 2-by-1/4-inch matchsticks24 little basil leaves2 scallions, minced2 tablespoons slashed unsalted boiled peanuts

Step by step instructions to make it

Light a grill. In a medium bowl, blend 1 tablespoon of the oil in with the fish sauce, lemongrass, five-zest powder, nectar, minced garlic, and 1/2 teaspoon of salt. Include the flank steak and hurl to cover.Utilizing scissors, clip off the stems from the grape leaves and spread a couple of the forgets about on a work surface. Spot 2 cuts of the garlic in the focal point of each leaf. Top with 2 cuts of steak, 2 bits of jicama, and 2 basil leaves. Fold up the leaves into tight chambers, taking care of the sides as you roll. Rehash with the rest of the grape leaves, garlic, steak, jicama, and basil. String the moves onto 4 pairs of sticks, with the goal that each pair holds 3 rolls. Daintily brush the pierced steps with oil.In a little skillet, heat the staying 1/4 cup of oil until only starting to smoke. Expel from the warmth and include the scallions and 1/2 teaspoon of salt. Quickly empty the hot scallion oil into a ramekin.Grill the turns over reasonably high warmth, turning once, until daintily singed outside and firm, around 8 minutes. Move the moves to a platter and sprinkle the scallion oil on top. Sprinkle with the peanuts and serve.

Grilled Tomato Crostini

Ingredients
- Four 3/4-inch-thick cuts of crusty bread1 garlic clove, dividedJuicy Grilled TomatoesOlive oil, for sprinklingSalt20 little basil leaves

How to Make It
Light a grill or preheat a grill container. Grill the crusty bread until toasted and seared in spots, around 1 moment for every side. Move to plates and rub them with the garlic parts. Spoon the tomatoes and their juices over the grilled bread and sprinkle with olive oil. Sprinkle with salt and basil and serve.

Spiced Shrimp and Tomato Kebabs

This is an ideal gathering dish since it's so natural to collect, and you can marinate and stick the shrimp early.

Ingredients
- 1/4 cup meagerly cut stripped ginger4 garlic cloves1/4 cup pressed cilantro leaves2 tablespoons pressed basil leaves1 tablespoon pressed mint leaves1 teaspoon cayenne1 teaspoon smoked paprika2 tablespoons lime juice2 teaspoons honey2 teaspoons salt2 tablespoons extra-virgin olive oil, in addition to additional for brushing40 enormous shrimp (around 2 pounds), shelled and deveined1-pint grape tomatoes

The most effective method to make it
In a food processor, consolidate the ginger with the garlic, cilantro, basil, mint, cayenne, paprika, lime juice, nectar, salt and the 2 tablespoons of olive oil and puree. Scratch the marinade into a considerable bowl, add the shrimp and hurl to cover. Cover and refrigerate for in any event 30 minutes or for as long as 4 hours.String the shrimp and tomatoes onto sticks.Light a grill and oil the meshes. Grill the sticks over high warmth, turning once, until the shrimp are gently roasted and cooked through and the tomatoes are merely starting to blast around 6 minutes. Serve immediately.

Grilled Apricot, Arugula, and Goat Cheese Salad

For this enjoyment go between a plate of mixed greens and a cheese course, grills apricots to give them a pleasant smokiness, at that point serves them with goat cheese, arugula, and a toasted–pine nut dressing.

Ingredients

- 6 crisp apricots, split and pitted3 tablespoons extra-virgin olive oil1 teaspoon thyme leavesSalt and naturally ground pepper2 tablespoons pine nuts1 1/2 teaspoons matured balsamic vinegar1 bundle (4 ounces) arugula, stemmedOne 4-ounce log crisp goat cheese, cut into 12 slices

Step by step instructions to make it

Light a grill. In a medium bowl, hurl the apricots with 1 tablespoon of the olive oil and the thyme and season with salt and pepper. Let represent 10 minutes.Grill the apricot parts over high warmth for around 5 minutes, turning once, until daintily scorched and mellowed.In the interim, in a little skillet, toast the pine nuts over moderate warmth, mixing, until brilliant, around 3 minutes. Move the nuts to a cutting board and finely cleave.Put the pine nuts in a medium bowl. Rush in the vinegar and the staying 2 tablespoons of olive oil and season with salt and pepper. Include the arugula and hurl. Orchestrate the goat cheese cuts on plates. Top with the apricot parts and arugula plate of mixed greens and serve immediately.

Pork Satay

Pork satay, a staple among vendors in Singapore, usually is exceptionally sweet. It marinates in a mix of lemongrass and coconut milk, is progressively adjusted. He additionally includes additional fennel seeds, making the delicate speared meat significantly increasingly fragrant.

Ingredients

- 3 huge shallots, cleaved (3/4 cup)1/4 cup unsweetened coconut milk2 full crisp lemongrass stalks, delicate internal bulbs just, hacked1 Fresno chile, cleaved2 Brazil nuts or macadamia nuts, squashed1 tablespoon palm sugar or light darker sugar1 1/2 teaspoons ground fennel seeds1/2 teaspoon squashed red pepper1/2 teaspoon naturally ground dark pepper1/2 teaspoon shrimp glue (see Note) or anchovy glueKosher salt1 tablespoon vegetable oil, in addition to additional for brushing1 pound of pork shoulder, cut into 1-by-1/4-inch strips1 teaspoon granulated sugarLime wedges, for serving

Step by step instructions to make it

In a food processor, join the shallots, coconut milk, lemongrass, chili, nuts, palm sugar, fennel seeds, squashed red pepper, dark pepper, shrimp glue, 1/2 teaspoon of salt and the 1 tablespoon of oil. Process until a glue structure.In a considerable bowl, hurl the pork strips with the shallot glue, 1 teaspoon of salt and the granulated sugar. Spread with saran wrap and refrigerate medium-term.Soak 12 bamboo sticks in water for in any event 30 minutes. Light a grill. String the pork onto the rods, brush with vegetable oil and season with salt. Grill over moderate warmth, turning once in a while until gently scorched and simply cooked through, around 10 minutes. Move the pork sticks to a platter and present with lime wedges.

Grilled Oysters with Chorizo Butter

Ingredients

- 4 ounces crisp Mexican chorizo, housings evacuated1 1/2 sticks unsalted margarine, cut into 1/2-inch blocks2 tablespoons fresh lime juiceSalt18 Louisiana or another medium to enormous clams, cleanedCilantro leaves and finely ground lime pizzazz, for decorating

The most effective method to prepare it

Cook the chorizo over moderate warmth, separating it with a spoon, until delicately seared, 8 minutes. Scratch into a bowl and let cool, at that point, break into little clusters.Add a tablespoon of water to the skillet and stew over low warmth. Add the margarine to the skillet a couple of solid shapes one after another, whisking continually until liquefied before including more. Mix in the chorizo and lime squeeze and season with salt. Keep warm over little warmth.Light a grill. Spot the clams on the grill, level side up. Grill over high warmth until the shells open slightly. Cautiously move to a platter and, utilizing kitchen gloves or a glove, evacuate the top crust. Spoon the chorizo margarine onto the shellfish and trimming with a cilantro leaf and lime zest. Serve immediately.

CHAPTER FIVE GRILLED RECIPES FOR VEGETARIAN, FISH, AND SEAFOODS

Grilled Eggplant, Roasted Red Pepper Sandwich, and Halloumi

These delicious grilled eggplant, broiled red pepper, and halloumi sandwiches are an extraordinary method to appreciate late summers produce!

Ingredients

- oilsalt and pepper1 medium eggplant, cut 1/4 inch thick8 cups of bread8 ounces of halloumi, sliced 1/4 inch thick2 simmered red peppers, cut into 4 cuts2 cups serving of mixed greens2 enormous beefsteak tomatoes, sliced 1/4 inch thick4 tablespoons basil pesto1/2 lemon, juiced

Directions

Lightly brush the eggplant and bread with oil and season the eggplant with salt and pepper.Grill the eggplant over medium-high warmth until delicate, around 2-4 minutes for every side.Lightly grill the bread and halloumi on the two hands and afterward hit the halloumi with the lemon juice.Assemble the sandwiches and appreciate it!

Grilled Tofu Tacos with Avocado Cashew Cream

My vegetarian view on a fish taco, these tofu tacos are smoky, fiery, tart, and delightful! Vegan and gluten-free with gluten-free corn tortilla

IngredientsFor the marinated tofu:

- 1 square extra-firm tofu, cut about ¼-inch thick3 tablespoons extra-virgin olive oilJuice and get-up-and-go of 1 lime1 garlic clove, minced½ teaspoon agave¼ teaspoon onion powder (or a couple of tablespoons of a new minced onion)¼ teaspoon paprika¼ teaspoon chipotle¼ teaspoon cuminSea salt and fresh black pepper

For the red cabbage slaw:

- ½ cup daintily cut red cabbage1-2 teaspoons rice or white wine vinegar1-2 teaspoons lime juiceSea saltSplash agave or squeeze sugar (discretionary)

For the avocado cashew cream:
- ½ cup crude, unsalted cashews½ cup of waterJuice of 1 lime (a couple of tablespoons)1 little avocado½ cooked jalapeño (slash up the other half as a feature of your taco filling)Sea salt½ teaspoon agave (discretionary)Splash white wine vinegar, to temper zest (discretionary)

To assemble:
- TortillasGrilled or cooked corn (I simmered corn simultaneously I was roasting my jalapeño, it might require less time, however simply watch it, it's generous).Chopped jalapeños held from the sauce above

Instructions

Sprinkle the tofu cuts with a liberal measure of salt, place them between 2 towels, and put something substantial on top (a couple of overwhelming books or a huge pot with individual jars in it will do). Let sit for about 30 minutes or so to deplete out a portion of the dampness.Mix the marinade: In a little bowl, whisk together the olive oil, lime squeeze and get-up-and-go, garlic, agave, onion powder, paprika, chipotle, cumin, and salt and pepper. After squeezing the tofu, cut it into square shapes, and spot it in a rimmed dish huge enough for the tofu to fit in one layer. Pour on the marinade and flip the tofu to cover the two sides. Put in a safe spot while you set up different ingredients.Make the red cabbage slaw: In a little bowl, blend the cut cabbage in with the vinegar, lime squeeze, a touch of salt, and a sprinkle of agave, whenever wanted. Let sit, chilling in the ice chest for 15-20 minutes or until you're prepared to serve. Taste and alter flavoring.Make the avocado cashew cream: In a high-speed blender, consolidate the cashews, water, lime juice, avocado, cooked jalapeño, salt, and agave, if utilizing. Mix until smooth. Taste and alter flavoring, including a sprinkle of white wine vinegar if it's excessively fiery. Chill in the ice chest for 15-20 minutes, or until you're prepared to serve.Remove the tofu from the marinade and grill 1-2 minutes for each side – a grilled dish is okay on the off chance that you don't have an outside grill.Remove the tofu from warm and pour on the rest of the marinade for additional flavor. (You can do this here because this is tofu and not fish or meat – don't reuse the marinade in case you're grilling fish or meat).Fill the tortillas with the tofu, cabbage slaw, avocado cashew cream, corn, saved jalapeño, or fixings of your decision.

Grilled Eggplant with Herbed Quinoa

The sumac in za'atar offers a tad of smokiness that praises the grilled flavor. You could utilize millet or another entire grain if you have something different available. The accompanying gives you more eggplant to quinoa proportion, but if you incline toward it the other way, just double the quinoa salad

instructions

- 3-4 medium eggplants (possibly two bigger ones, four littler ones)sea saltextra virgin olive oilza'atar flavoring1/2 cup quinoa, washedhalf of a little red onion, cut slimgenerous bunch every one of crisp basil, dill, and cilantro2 Tbsp. escapades, generally cleaved1 Tbsp. additional virgin olive oil2 Tbsp. red wine vinegar2 tsp. honey or agave nectar1/3 cup toasted pine nuts

Instructions

Cut the eggplants into 1/2" adjusts. Sprinkle with salt and put in a safe spot for 30 minutes to discharge water.Put the quinoa in a pot with a spot of salt and 3/4 cup water or stock. Carry it to a delicate bubble, spread, and cook for 15 minutes. Mood killer the warmth, cushion with a fork, spread again, and leave it to steam an additional 5 minutes.Warmth up your grill or grill container. Press the eggplants between a dishcloth or paper towels to ingest the abundance dampness. Brush the two sides with olive oil and grill for around 5 minutes for each side until you get decent dull imprints, and the surface appears to be entirely delicate all through. I like the gentler surface that accompanies covering them. Expel to a plate, shower more olive oil and sprinkle with za'atar to taste.To complete the quinoa, hurl in the onions, the entirety of the herbs, oil, vinegar, nectar or agave, and a liberal spot of salt and pepper. Hurl to blend. Taste and change as you wish.Put the eggplants in a plate, top with the quinoa, and trimming with the toasted pine nuts.

Grilled Tofu and Soba Noodles Recipe

Ingredients

- 12 ounces/340g dried soba noodles2 teaspoons extra-virgin olive oil, in addition to more for the tofu16 oz/450g extra-firm tofu, depleted and tapped dry3 medium cloves garlicinsufficient 3/4 teaspoon exceptional grain ocean salt3 little/medium shallots3 small serrano peppers, minced1 bundle (around 4 bunches) of cilantro, stems cut1 teaspoon genuine sweetener (or darker sugar)2 teaspoons crisp lime juice1 cup/170 ml extra-virgin olive oil

Instructions

Heat a huge pot of water to the point of boiling. Salt liberally, at that point, cook the soba noodles per bundle instructions, being careful not to overcook them. Channel, run under virus water for a moment, shake of however much additional water as could reasonably be expected, at that point hurl well with the olive oil. Delicately work the olive oil through the noodles. Spot the soba in a considerable plastic pack and refrigerate medium-term, or until you're prepared to utilize them - up to a couple of days.Make the dressing utilizing a mortar and pestle OR a food processor. I used the map, which takes some time (and gives an incredible arm exercise), yet I incline toward the final product. Pound the garlic and salt into a glue, at that point work in the shallots each in turn, at that point the peppers. At that point, the cilantro a bunch at once. The blend ought to be very smooth. Include the sugar, at that point, the lime squeeze before blending in the olive oil a piece at once. Taste and change the flavors if need be - progressively salt, sugar, lime juice, and so on utilizing the processor? Simply mix everything. At that point, change the flavors a piece if necessary.Cut the tofu into pieces (see photograph), rub delicately with olive oil, and spot-on a medium-hot grill. Cook until brilliant dark colored on one side, flip, and grill the opposite side too.To collect, hurl the soba noodles with a decent measure of the dressing, holding enough to sprinkle liberally over the tofu. Spot the tofu over the noodles, and shower with all the more dressing.

Fish and Seafood Grilled Onion-Butter Cod

This delectably grilled cod has a phenomenal, rich flavor and surface. The onion and white wine join with the margarine to make a smooth sauce that, albeit easy to make, will taste as though you went through hours making it. Presented with your preferred grilled potatoes or vegetable of your decision, this dish makes the ideal weeknight meal or great course for an uncommon social affair.

Ingredients

- 1/4 cup margarine1 little onion (finely slashed)1/4 cup white wine4 (6-ounce) cod fillets1 tablespoon extra-virgin olive oil1/2 teaspoon salt (or to taste)1/2 teaspoon dark pepperLemon wedges (for serving)

Instructions

Gather the ingredients.Preheat grill to medium-high warmth.In small skillet soften spread. Include onions and cook for 1 to 2 minutes.Add white wine and let stew for an extra 3 minutes. Expel from warmth and let cool for 5 minutes.Brush filets with extra-virgin olive oil and sprinkle with salt and pepper. Place fish on a well-oiled grill rack and cook for 8 minutes.Baste cod with spread sauce and cautiously flip over fish. Cook for an extra 7 minutes, seasoning fish aggregate of 2 to multiple times, or until fish is murky, chips effectively with a fork, and arrives at an inside temperature of 145 F.Remove cod from the grill, top with lemon wedges, and serve.

Tips

- It is normal to be anxious about cooking fish fillets on the grill. The fish can undoubtedly self-destruct and sneak past the meshes, or it can adhere to the grill making it practically difficult to turn in one piece. It is imperative to oil the grill grinds very well before cooking a bit of fish and to have a large grilling spatula close by. You should just flip the fish once and disregard it to cook the remainder of the time.Another choice is to utilize a grilling fish crate. The handles make turning the fish over about easy.To abstain from flipping the fish, grill it on a wooden plank.Wrapping the fish in a foil parcel is a straightforward and wreckage free system that will bestow a smoky grill season, yet the fish won't get any grill marks.Store any extra cooked fish in an airtight holder in the fridge for as long as 3 days after introductory cooking. Drop any scraps and add to soups or stews.

Moroccan Grilled Fish Kebabs

Kebabs are an incredible method to appreciate meat, seafood, or potentially vegetables on the grill. These Moroccan-spiced fish kebabs are anything but difficult to make and carry profundity of flavor to any white fish. The paprika, turmeric, bean stew powder, garlic, and cilantro include both shading and flavor. You can serve these fish kebabs without anyone else's input as appetizers, or serve them over rice with grilled vegetables for a total meal.

Ingredients

- 1 1/2 pounds firm white fish1 cup red onion (slashed)1/3 cup olive oil2 tablespoons cilantro (finely cut)3 tablespoons crisp lemon juice1 teaspoon paprika1 teaspoon salt1/2 teaspoon turmeric1/2 teaspoon dark pepper1/2 teaspoon stew powder2 cloves garlic (minced)

Steps to Make It

Cut fish into 1-inch squares. Spot pieces in a resealable plastic sack.In a little bowl, place the remaining ingredients and mix to consolidate. Empty this blend into the pack with fish. Seal pack, pivot to blend thoroughly, and permit to marinate in the fridge for 30 minutes.Preheat grill to medium-high warmth. Expel fish from the sack and dispose of the marinade. String fish into sticks.Place the fish kebabs on the grill and cook on medium-high warmth for 10 minutes, turning sometimes. When fish turns dark and drops effectively and arrives at an inside temperature of 145 to 150 F, expel from the grill and serve.

Tips

You can utilize wood or metal sticks to make the kabobs. If you are using wooden sticks, make a point to absorb them water for at any rate an hour prior to stringing fish to abstain from consuming them on the grill.When picking a fish for this recipe, ensure you select one that is substantial and firm; a slight, fragile fish (like fumble or sole) will self-destruct either while attempting to string onto the sticks or on the grill. Significant kinds of fish to pick are swordfish, halibut, mahi-mahi, striped bass, yellowtail snapper, monkfish, and kingfish.It will be simpler to cut the fish into solid shapes if you buy fish steaks. On the off chance that you plan to purchase a more slender fish, ensure it has its skin as this will help keep the fish flawless. It is additionally imperative to cut the fish into equivalent measured solid shapes, so the entirety of the pieces cook in a similar measure of time.While stringing onto the stick, make sure to leave space between each bit of fish. It will cook increasingly slow if the food is contacting one another. Additionally, make a point to marinate the fish blocks no longer than 30 minutes as the corrosive in the lime juice can start to separate the tissue or even begin to cook the fish.

Grilled Bacon-Wrapped Scallops with Lemon Aioli

A mixed drink party top choice, bacon-wrapped scallops are easy to get ready and straightforward to eat (particularly while holding a beverage). The substantial scallop enclosed by a portion of bacon is delightful all alone however is taken to another level when presented with lemon aioli for plunging. This recipe is immaculate served without anyone else as an hors d'oeuvre, or it very well may be made into a flavorful backup to any plate of mixed greens. Ingredients

- 2 tablespoons red wine vinegar2 tablespoons olive oilDash dark pepper, or to taste2 pounds huge new scallops8 cuts of baconFor the Aioli:1/2 cup mayonnaise1 tablespoon lemon get-up-and-go (get-up-and-go of 1 medium lemon)1 tablespoon new lemon juice1 clove garlic (minced)1 teaspoon Dijon mustardDash salt, or to taste1 tablespoon level leaf parsley (finely hacked)

Steps to Make It

Combine vinegar, oil, and dark pepper in a medium bowl. Add scallops to the blend and hurl to cover. Cover and permit to sit for 5 to 10 minutes at room temperature.Preheat grill to medium-high warmth. Cut bacon into thirds. Fold a bit of bacon over each scallop and string onto sticks. There ought to be 3 to 4 scallops for each stick.Place sticks on a gently oiled grill rack and cooks for 3 to 4 minutes for each side. At the point when the scallop is misty in shading, expel from the grill.To get ready, lemon aioli, in a medium bowl, join mayonnaise with lemon pizzazz, lemon juice, garlic, mustard, salt, pepper, and parsley. Mix to join and present with bacon-wrapped scallops. The recipe can be multiplied if necessary. On the off chance that creation early, spread the bowl with saran wrap and place in the fridge.

Tip

- This recipe just works with huge scallops or ocean scallops. Cove scallops are too little even to consider preparing like this.

Tuna Chops with Lemon Cream Sauce

In this recipe, crisp yellowfin fish hacks are dressed with a simple container sauce of lemon cream and tricks. Take care not to demolish your venture by overcooking the fish. Have your ingredients arranged and all set, and you can have this on the table in around 15 minutes.Ingredients

- 8 oz fish (2 crisp yellowfin steaks)Kosher salt (to taste)Freshly ground dark pepper (to taste)1 teaspoon olive oil2 tablespoons margarine (isolated use)1/8 cup onions (sweet, crisp, minced)1 clove garlic (finely minced)1/4 cup white wine1 teaspoon lemon juice (crisp, or more to taste)1/4 cup cream (substantial)2 tablespoons capers (depleted)Garnish: crisp dill weed and lemon or lime wedges

Steps to Make It

Sprinkle both sides yellowfin fish steaks with suitable salt and newly ground pepper.Heat a substantial skillet over high warmth. Include olive oil and 1 tablespoon of the spread, and twirl to cover the skillet. Burn fish steaks until brilliant dark colored on each side, turning just once. Try not to overcook fish. Evacuate and keep warm.Lower warmth to medium. Include the rest of the tablespoon of margarine to the skillet alongside the onions. Tenderly sauté until onions are translucent. Include garlic and sauté 1 extra moment, mixing frequently. Cautiously pour in the white wine and lemon juice. Mix and cook until the fluid is decreased considerably, around 2 to 3 minutes. Include overwhelming cream, come back to a stew. Cook an additional 3 minutes or so until thickened. Mix in depleted tricks.Pour lemon cream sauce over warm fish steaks, and embellishment with dill and lemon or lime to serve.

Grilled Dungeness Crab

The grill adds incredible flavor to any sort of seafood. This recipe for grilled Dungeness crab is straightforward, yet very flavorful. You'll have these prepared rapidly and have sufficient opportunity to eat and associate with your visitors. This recipe subtleties how to grill crisp live crabs. Be that as it may, those aren't generally in season, and in any event, when they are, you may need the comfort of having another person bubble them for you. If the idea of live crabs is a lot for you, at that point, buy solidified crabs. Simply ensure they are decent and defrosted before putting them on the grill. Solidified crab can defrost medium-term in the fridge, or you can put it in a holder of cool water for an hour or somewhere in the vicinity. But if you are picking live crabs, the ones you need are those that are dynamic and caution. The slow ones are probably going to be less solid and less scrumptious — the bigger, the better to give increasingly tasty crab meat. Ingredients

- 1/4 cup/120 ml white wine vinegar3 tablespoons/15 ml of sugar2 tablespoons/30 ml olive oil1 tablespoon/15 ml ginger (minced)1 jalapeño stew (minced with the seeds evacuated)3 clove garlic (squashed)1 tablespoon/15 ml cilantro (minced)2 huge Dungeness crabs (live)

Steps to Make It

Gather the ingredients. To set up the treat, blend vinegar, sugar, oil, ginger, jalapeño, garlic, and cilantro in a bowl. Spread and put in a safe spot. Drop the crabs, each in turn, carelessly into the bubbling water. Bubble, at that point, diminish the warmth and let stew for 5 minutes. Remove crabs from the water. Pull off the triangular tab from the tummy. Liftoff the shell. Clean innards and gills from crab and wash and channel. Pat dry with paper towels. Preheat grill for medium-high warmth. Place the crabs on the grill. Cook with the top shut, brushing with treating blend after initial 2 to 3 minutes of cooking. Turn crabs over part of the way through grilling, and process once more. The crabs are done when the meat in the leg is misty, which will take around 10 to 12 minutes. Place the crab on a serving dish and spoon remaining seasoning blend over the crabs. You can supplant the shells before serving if you wish. Serve with lemon wedges and drawn margarine, as wanted.

Tip

- Be sure to have the entirety of the crab-eating utensils (wafers and pick forks) helpful for your visitors so they can select the whole of the delicious crab meat. Face cloths and additional napkins will be required, in addition to access to hand washing offices after the crab picking and eating is finished. You'll additionally need dishes, a bowl, or a can for them to store the shells. There are probably not going to be any remains, yet if there are, you should save the crab in the more relaxed and appreciate it inside a day.

Grilled Sea Bass Marinated

This basic grilled sea bass dish to plan. Since you can marinate the fish medium-term, this makes it an extraordinary plan ahead meal.Ingredients

- 4 bits of ocean bass, around 4 to 6 ounces each1/2 cup/120 mL purpose1/4 cup/60 mL oil2 tablespoons/30 mL soy sauce2 tablespoons/30 mL sugar2 tablespoons/30 mL crisp ginger (minced)2 cloves garlic (minced)1 teaspoon/5 mL dark pepper

Steps to Make It

Place ocean bass pieces in a shallow glass dish.In a little bowl, join all marinade ingredients.Pour blend over fish, spread, and permit to marinate in the fridge for 3 to 12 hours.Preheat grill for medium-high warmth.Remove fish from the glass dish and dispose of the marinade.The place the fish on the grill and cook for about 12 minutes, turning once.When fish is obscure and drops effectively, expel from the warmth and serve.

Lime and Basil Tilapia Recipe

The mix of lime and basil truly adds flavor to the tilapia. This dish can either be eaten alongside grilled vegetables or cut and served in tacos or over rice.Ingredients

- 4 tilapia filets (around 1 pound)1/4 cup olive oil2 tablespoons lime juiceZest of 2 limes1 tablespoon new basil, minced2 teaspoons whiskey1 teaspoon saltBlack pepper to taste

Steps to Make It

Combine olive oil, lime juice, lime get-up-and-go, crisp basil, whiskey, salt, and dark pepper in a little bowl. Spot tilapia fillets in a resealable plastic sack and pour marinade over the top. Ensure all surfaces are covered well with the marinade. Seal sack and more relaxed for 30 minutes.Preheat grill for medium-high warmth.Remove fish from the pack and dry marinade into a pot. Heat marinade to the point of boiling, quickly diminish the warmth, and let stew on low for 5 minutes. Expel from warmth, spread, and keep warm.Grill tilapia filets for 3 to 5 minutes for every side over high heat. At the point when fish arrives at an inward temperature of 145 F. furthermore, it seems dark in shading, expel from the grill, and present with a couple of spoonful's of marinade showered over the top.If utilizing the fish for tacos. Avoid the last step and brush the tilapia with the cooked marinade as it cooks. Expel from heat once done and chip into reduced down pieces.

Grilled Scallops with Mango/Peaches and Red Bell Pepper

Attempt this Thai recipe for Grilled Scallops. Either crisp mango or peaches can be utilized, contingent upon what is new and accessible where you live. Either ocean scallops or bigger narrows scallops can be used in this recipe, and both are similarly wonderful. As a little something extra, a similar method for the marinade serves as a sauce that you spoon over just before eating, making this scallops recipe essential only as bright and gourmet-delightful. Ideal for a picnic or grill party.Ingredients

- 6 to 8 ocean scallops OR 10-14 cove scallops (enough for 2 individuals)1 to 2 mangoes (cut into enormous lumps, OR 3 peaches (natural product ought to be ready yet at the same time firm))1 immense red ringer pepperFor the Marinade:4 tbsp. lime (juice of 2 limes)4 tbsp. fish sauce (accessible in tall jugs at Asian food stores)4 tbsp. oil, (for example, coconut or canola)2 tsp. garlic1/2 cup crisp coriander (slashed)1 crunchy red bean stew (deseeded and minced, OR 1/2 tsp. cayenne pepper)1/2 tsp. coarsely-ground dark pepper2 storing tsp. more colored sugar (not pressed)Optional: 1 to 2 tsp. margarine

Steps to Make It

Rinse the scallops under cold water. Pat dry and place in an enormous blending bowl.Cut the mango or peaches and red ringer pepper into lumps approximating the size of the scallops (for ocean scallops, you need huge pieces). Spot these in the bowl with the scallops.Place all the marinade ingredients (except the margarine) together in a pan. Mix well to make a slim, however delicious marinade.Pour a portion of the marinade over the scallops, mango or peaches, and pepper, delicately mixing it in. Leave the rest of the pan.Allow scallops, organic products, and pepper to marinate for around 10 minutes (no longer than 15). In the interim, heat your grill/grill.Gently lance the scallops together with the foods grown from the ground pepper. You can either stick the scallops through the inside or through the sides (side-skewering works better for cooking).Before baking, rapidly brush your grill with a little vegetable oil to forestall staying.Cook the sticks over a hot grill for 10 to 15 minutes. Brush with a tad bit of the remaining marinade from the base of the bowl the first couple of times you turn them. You can likewise sprinkle with somewhat more dark pepper.The sticks are done when scallops are daintily caramelized, and the peach and red pepper are mollified. Scallops are done when firm up and are dark (not translucent) in the inside.Warm up the pot containing the held marinade over medium warmth. This solitary takes 30 seconds to 1 moment, just until warm - any more extended will pulverize the taste. Whenever wanted, include a little spread. At the point when the range melts, mix the sauce, and it's prepared!Taste-test the sauce, including more sugar if unreasonably sharp for your taste, or more lime/lemon if excessively sweet or excessively salty.Serve the scallop sticks with rice, and a portion of the sauce spooned over. Or then again, you can utilize the sauce as a plunge if eating the scallop sticks individually.

Cilantro Lime Fish Halibut

This halibut is treated in a rich margarine sauce stacked with incredible flavor. You can serve this grilled fish without anyone else's input or use it in servings of mixed greens or fish tacos.Ingredients

- 4 halibut steaks (1-inch thick)3/4 cup/180 mL new cilantro (finely slashed)1/4 cup/60 mL spread3 tablespoons/45 mL new lime juice1 clove of garlic (minced)1/2 teaspoon/2.5 mL of red pepper chips1/2 teaspoon/2.5 mL of ocean salt1/2 teaspoon/2.5 mL of coarse dark pepperGarnish: 4 to 6 lime wedges

Steps to Make It

Gather the ingredients.Put the halibut in a baking dish and coat with lime juice. Sprinkle with salt and pepper and put it in a safe spot for 20 minutes.Meanwhile, soften margarine in a little pan over medium warmth. Include garlic and sauté for around one moment.Add cilantro and red pepper drops and mix for one moment. Expel from heat.Place halibut on the preheated grill over a medium-high fire. Grill until obscure through the middle, around 5 to 7 minutes for each side.Baste as often as possible with spread sauce while grilling. Present with lime wedges. Appreciate!

CHAPTER SIX ONE WEEK OF GRILLED MEAL PLAN

What's Included

- 100% authentic food grilling recipes that are straightforward, straight-forward, and family amicable.All of the recipes are anything but difficult to make and can normally be made in less than 60 minutes.This one-week plan is very meat substantial and utilizes the grill. Every recipe can be cooked in the kitchen OR on the grill. Try not to feel restricted on the off chance that you don't have a grill.

What's Not Included

- This plan isn't attached to a particular market or value point. Not every person approaches the markdown supermarketsSpices, oils, and vinegar. We're not utilizing colossal measures of any of these in this meal plan (except bean stew powder), and you most likely as of now have these cooking staples at any rate.Corn starch or any modest quantities of flour. Once more, these are cooking staples, and we're not utilizing a lot.Precautions for food sensitivities.

No Breakfasts or Lunches?

This meal plan does exclude any breakfast or lunch recipes because, as far as I can tell, most of the families have individual inclinations on what they need for breakfast or lunch. No stresses. However – I have no uncertainty about the ingredients you purchase for this meal plan will give additional items that you can use to cover breakfasts as well as snacks. Here's the reason:

- Every meal on this menu is something I frequently make with my family. Every one of them covers supper for the four of us AND enough for in any event one extra lunch (typically two). Use the "Reward Meal Ideas" area at the base to make your very own breakfast and lunch menu. Those are only a few plans to kick you off, yet they're there to assist you with utilizing the ingredients you're as of now purchasing! If, regardless, you don't think this is sufficient food to cover breakfast and snacks, buy a sack of apples and a holder of oatmeal for breakfast and just put a couple of more dollars on your bill!

Uncommon Notes Regarding This Grilling Meal Plan:

- Even however, this is a grilling meal plan, the entirety of the meals can be cooked in your kitchen all the way. A portion of the meals expect you to begin at the stove; however, none of them have you turn on the oven. This meal plan is nonstop. This implies a portion of the food arranged before in the week will be utilized later in the week. Be cautious if you choose to make the meals in another request. I'm not saying you need to follow the plan precisely, simply know different pieces of a meal are thought to be prepared when you find a workable pace. For instance, the Teriyaki Chicken Lettuce Wrap recipe expects you previously made the chicken and Cabbage Slaw on one more day – so you should simply gather!

What to Buy

The objective with any plan is to purchase as little food as could be expected under the circumstances, use all that you are buying, and do both without yielding taste or quality. This is what you're buying for this meal plan:

Produce

Carrots. These will be utilized in the Grilled Vegetable foil pack on day 1. Foil packs are one of my preferred things since they are a cooking vessel AND plate! Simple tidy up all around!**Grape Tomatoes.** In your foil packs and servings of mixed greens will be your grape tomatoes. While these can be on the costly side, dividing them causes them to go further, and they are so acceptable cooked.**Zucchini.** Zucchini will likewise be in the foil packs alongside a great recipe straight on the grill: Grilled Lemon-Salt Zucchini.**Cucumber.** A refreshing expansion to your nursery and side plate of mixed greens.**Garlic Cloves.** Most of these will be in an astonishing stew! Try not to hold back on the garlic, and it includes an incredible flavor.**Green Cabbage.** Green cabbage is so flexible and adds an incredible smash to the Sweet Potato "Tacos" and Teriyaki Chicken Lettuce Wraps as Cabbage Slaw.**Green Onions**. These go effectively with the Teriyaki Grilled Chicken Kabobs on day 5. Ensure you don't toss out those white stems since you can utilize them in Bonus Meal Ideas later.**Jalapeño.** You will utilize the Jalapeno to add some zest to the Sweet Potato "Tacos," don't hesitate to preclude on the off chance that you would prefer to hold the warmth down (or twofold if you like it hot!).**Lemon.** Lemon is the superstar in two or three meals this week: Grilled Lemon Honey Chicken and Grilled Lemon-Salt Zucchini. You will have some remaining juice that you can in a rewarding recipe, so don't dispose of those lemons!**Onion (white).** We go somewhat overwhelming on the onions this week, so make sure to include the number clinched or purchase two sacks.**Iceberg Lettuce.** The modest alternative for a Side Salad and Garden Salad that utilizes remaining Grilled Lemon Honey Chicken. I love to add a chunk of ice side plates of mixed greens to lighter meals to guarantee full tummies and bunches of veggies while adhering to my spending limit.

Red Leaf Lettuce. I as of late went over this alternative at the store due to the absence of accessibility of romaine lettuce. The leaves are pleasant and large and fall to pieces flawlessly – ideal for Teriyaki Chicken Lettuce Wraps.**Russets Potatoes**. Russets are light in this meal plan, yet regardless I prescribe purchasing a 5 to 10 lb. pack (you just need 2 1/2 lbs.) since they are so flexible and modest! Pure oven hash tans are the base to an astounding Spinach and Bacon Quiche on day 6.**Spinach.** One sack of crisp spinach could do the stunt here (you just need 3 cups); however, on the off chance that a bundle is less expensive, you could generally add the remaining spinach to your servings of mixed greens for the week.**Sweet Corn**. We aren't in corn season yet. However, I don't figure I could have a Grilled Vegetable Foil Pack without some buttered corn :)**Sweet Peppers**. Any kind of peppers will work here; however, green is the cheapest decision (and it tastes incredible as well!).**Sweet Potatoes**. The star Sweet Potato "Tacos." Tacos are prepared and ate from foil packs with heavenly Cabbage Slaw on top. No tortilla or plate required!

Cold Case/Dairy

Butter. I don't think it's feasible for me to make a plan without spread! In this plan, margarine is the primary oil in the Grilled Vegetable Foil Pack. Like I said previously, this plan can't be finished without corn and spread. (Also, margarine IS beneficial for you.)**Cheddar Cheese**. Scrumptious fixing for the Spinach and Bacon Quiche.**Egg**. Just about six eggs required here. You could buy the correct sum you need (if your store offers a ½ dozen choice) or get an entire dozen and go through some Bonus Meal Ideas.**Greek Yogurt**. This is the base for cabbage slaws. I like to utilize plain whole-milk Greek yogurt, and keeping in mind that it very well may be tart all alone, it isn't tyrannical in this slaw by any stretch of the imagination.**Milk.** This is utilized in the Spinach and Bacon Quiche and the Skillet Cornbread that goes close by a great Chili.

Pantry

Black Beans. While dry, dark beans are less expensive, it is as yet modest to buy canned beans. The sort you buy won't influence your meal by any stretch of the imagination, and it's everything up to individual inclination (and time).**Chili Powder**. I don't ordinarily incorporate flavors, yet the Chili recipe calls for ¼ cup of stew powder. While this seems like a great deal (I, however, it was a grammatical error), it isn't overpowering or unreasonably fiery for the healthy eater.**Cornmeal**. This exceptional fixing is for the skillet chile cake. No compelling reason to warm up the kitchen when you can cook cornbread on the grill!Diced Tomatoes. These diced tomatoes give the bean stew a decent consistency.**Dijon Mustard**. I don't regularly incorporate mustards, yet they are significant in the current week's chicken dishes.**Honey**. This sweet fixing is utilized in a few meals this week, Grilled Honey Lemon Chicken and Grilled Teriyaki Chicken Kabobs. There are several thoughts on the most proficient method to go through any staying nectar in the Bonus Meal Ideas this week (if this thing is certainly not a staple in your kitchen and you don't know how to manage the extra).**Pickled Jalapeños or Green Chilis.** These canned jalapenos or green bean stews add a pleasant kick to the bean stew. I lean toward green bean stews.**Kidney Beans**. Similarly, as with dark beans, dry beans are less expensive than canned, yet the sort you choose to utilize at last boils down to individual inclination and your spending limit for the week.**Sesame Seeds**. While these are for embellishing, I think they likewise add a pleasant flavor to the Grilled Teriyaki Chicken Kabobs.**Soy Sauce**. In the event that you are, a soy-free family doesn't hesitate to sub coconut amines for the soy sauce. (Fluid amines are a decent choice as well.)

Tomato Sauce. Two recipes need tomato sauce this week – each with an alternate sum for the can (14 and 16oz). Whichever amount you find ought to be exceptional in every recipe.**Worcestershire Sauce**. This adds its exceptional flavor to the Grilled Lemon Honey Chicken on day 1 (remains on day 3!)**Brown Rice**. A simple filling expansion to the Teriyaki Grilled Chicken Kabobs and Grilled Lemon-Salt Zucchini – ideal for absorbing that yummy teriyaki sauce.

Meat

To keep my meals economical, I typically do exclude as a lot of meat as I did during the current week's meal plan. However, I couldn't leave behind the opportunity extra destroyed chicken can give to get one out of the kitchen.

Bacon. The other portion of the Spinach and Bacon Quiche supper on day 6.**Chicken Breasts**. There is much chicken in this meal plan, yet I made a point to switch things up, keep the flavors new and adjust the introduction to ensure you don't become weary of it before the weeks over. To get this going, on two nighttime's, you grill bosoms and kabobs, every one of those suppers incorporates additional chicken to be prepared nearby your customary meal (no extra time required!).A day or so later, we switch up the additional chicken and add it to a superb Grilled Lemon Honey Chicken Garden Salad and a Teriyaki Chicken Salad Wrap that is topped with remaining Cabbage Slaw. That implies two no-cook evenings all from two or three new bosoms on the grill!**Ground Beef**. The meat is utilized in the Chili and Sweet Potato Tacos. I usually use 1lb of ground hamburger in my bean stew; however, this recipe makes a lot of stew, so I utilize 2lbs to ensure it doesn't get lost with different ingredients.

One Week Grilling Meal Plan: Dinners

DAY 1: Grilled Lemon-Honey Chicken and Grilled Vegetable Foil Pack

DAY 2: Sweet Potato "Tacos" and Cabbage Slaw

DAY 3: Grilled Lemon Honey-Chicken Garden Salad

DAY 4: Chili and Skillet Cornbread

DAY 5: Teriyaki Grilled Chicken Kabobs and grilled Lemon-Salt Zucchini

DAY 6: Spinach and Bacon Quiche inside Salad

DAY 7: Teriyaki Chicken Lettuce Wraps

Meal Ideas Honey Roasted Carrots: (utilizing remaining nectar and carrots) + nothing extraMashed Potatoes: (remaining potatoes, milk and whites of the green onion)Grilled Cheese: (utilizing remaining Cheese) include breadHash Browns and Eggs: Using remaining eggs and vegetables (if you have any) for breakfast.Quiche: utilizing remaining eggs (include bacon, spinach, and hashtags)Salad Dressings: (using remaining Dijon, honey, and lemon juice) add olive oilYogurt and Banana Breakfast (using remaining Greek yogurt): add bananasVegetable Stock: Save vegetable finishes consistently (you can store them in old yogurt compartments or cooler packs) and make your vegetable stock.

www.ingramcontent.com/pod-product-compliance
Lightning Source LLC
Chambersburg PA
CBHW081120080526
44587CB00021B/3686